FOR ORGANS, PIANOS & ELECTRONIC KEYBOARDS

E-Z PLAY TODAY

140

THE ★ BEST ★ OF

GEORGE STRAIT
2ND EDITION

CONTENTS

Cover and interior photos by Mark Tucker

ISBN 978-0-7935-2454-9

HAL•LEONARD®
CORPORATION
7777 W. BLUEMOUND RD. P.O. BOX 13819 MILWAUKEE, WI 53213

Visit Hal Leonard Online at
www.halleonard.com

GEORGE STRAIT

Since George Strait's first MCA release in 1981, he has had no equal for consistency of quality, consistency of sales and influence on country music.

Every one of his 20 albums has been certified gold, platinum or multi-platinum, and Pure Country, the soundtrack from his 1992 movie, sold five million. His quadruple platinum boxed set, Strait Out of the Box, is the best selling country boxed set of all time, and is tied for second best selling in all genres with Led Zeppelin (surpassed only by Bruce Springsteen.) In cumulative record sales, SoundScan ranks Strait #10 among all artists since its 1992 inception, between Boyz II Men and Eric Clapton. A Louis Harris poll ranked him in the Top 10 of America's favorite singers on a list that included Frank Sinatra and Whitney Houston. His influence on country music is evident in an entire generation of "hat acts."

The most amazing part of Strait's career is that it's still on the rise. In *USA Today*, reviewer David Zimmerman summed up the feelings of many country fans when he wrote, "Sometimes you wonder: Is country music getting worse or is Strait just getting better and better?"

The record shows that George Strait is indeed just getting better and better. "Check Yes or No," the first single from his 1995 boxed set, Strait Out of the Box, did not just go to #1, it stayed at #1 for four weeks in Billboard and three weeks in R&R. "Carried Away," from his last album, Blue Clear Sky, spent a record-setting four weeks at #1 in Gavin, and the album entered Billboard's country album charts at #1. He won three Country Music Association awards in 1996, more than he has in any other year. His 1996 concerts broke attendance records set by Hank Williams Sr., Elvis Presley and several records previously set by (who else but?) George Strait.

The honesty and artistic integrity that is the foundation of George Strait's artistry has been there from the beginning. In an article in The Journal of Country Music, Don Daily of D Records, for whom Strait recorded in the 1970s, recalls that Strait "just got up there and sang real sincere."

Twenty years later, his co-producer Tony Brown measures his appeal by the effect he has on studio musicians. "It's just he does what he does, and the band falls in it," Brown said. "They don't play the same kind of licks they play on everybody else's records."

Strait has been playing the same kind of music ever since he formed his Ace In The Hole band in the 1970s. He had grown up in Pearsall, Texas, and gotten hooked on country music while stationed in the army in Hawaii. When he returned to Texas, he put together a band that, unlike most club bands, did not have any rock and pop music in their repertoire.

They never played anything but Texas dance hall music, and Strait could easily fill up an entire evening with Bob Wills songs if that's what the crowd wanted. However, in 1979, after several trips to Nashville yielded no major label recording contract, he decided to give up on music and take a job with a cattle-pen company. At the last minute, however, he decided to give music one more year.

Strait's manager Erv Woolsey, then an MCA executive, brought him to the attention of MCA, and his first MCA single, "Unwound," was released in 1981. In the Urban Cowboy era of packaged country music, country fans had no trouble recognizing the real thing when they heard it. Billboard magazine named Strait New Male Artist of the Year, and he would ultimately become the top male artist of the entire decade. He was named Male Vocalist of the Year twice by the Country Music Association in the '80s and three times by the Academy of Country Music. He took the CMA's top award, Entertainer of the Year, in 1989, and won the same award from both organizations in 1990.

Strait broadened his career in 1992 by starring in the film Pure Country, and the soundtrack became his biggest selling album. His 1995 boxed set, Strait Out of the Box, was a monumental collection of 72 cuts, ranging from 31 #1 singles to obscure, intriguing representations of his early days, all with rare personal comments from Strait himself. Eighteen of his albums are certified platinum (one million sold) or better, and his total sales now top 39 million albums.

Strait's success as a recording artist is matched by his live performances. In the 1990s, his concerts, which have always sold out, set records for how fast they sold out. He set a personal best in 1996, selling over 33,000 tickets for three shows in Phoenix in less than two hours. At the Astrodome he broke his own attendance record, playing to 125,000 people in two shows, and he's now played to over one million fans at the Astrodome's annual rodeo.

George Strait is Country Music's brightest and most enduring star, the classic voice of today reflecting the classic Country Music tradition of the past.

DISCOGRAPHY

Albums	Sales	Release Date
STRAIT COUNTRY	GOLD	9/4/81
STRAIT FROM THE HEART	GOLD	6/3/82
RIGHT OR WRONG	GOLD	10/6/83
DOES FT. WORTH EVER CROSS YOUR MIND [1]	PLATINUM	9/26/84
GREATEST HITS VOLUME I	TRIPLE PLATINUM	3/4/85
SOMETHING SPECIAL	PLATINUM	8/29/85
#7	PLATINUM	5/14/86
MERRY CHRISTMAS STRAIT TO YOU	PLATINUM	9/8/86
OCEAN FRONT PROPERTY [2]	PLATINUM	1/12/87
GREATEST HITS VOLUME II	TRIPLE PLATINUM	9/7/87
IF YOU AIN'T LOVIN' YOU AIN'T LIVIN'	PLATINUM	2/22/88
BEYOND THE BLUE NEON	PLATINUM	2/6/89
LIVIN' IT UP	PLATINUM	5/15/90
CHILL OF AN EARLY FALL	PLATINUM	3/19/91
TEN STRAIT HITS	PLATINUM	12/31/91
HOLDING MY OWN	PLATINUM	4/21/92
PURE COUNTRY	QUINTUPLE PLATINUM	9/15/92
EASY COME, EASY GO	DOUBLE PLATINUM	9/28/93
LEAD ON	PLATINUM	11/8/94
STRAIT OUT OF THE BOX	QUADRUPLE PLATINUM	9/12/95
BLUE CLEAR SKY [2,3]	DOUBLE PLATINUM	4/23/96
CARRYING YOUR LOVE WITH ME		4/22/97

1. 1985 CMA AND ACM ALBUM OF THE YEAR
2. DEBUTED #1 BILLBOARD
3. 1996 CMA ALBUM OF THE YEAR

SINGLES	PEAK BILLBOARD POSITION	RELEASE DATE
Unwound	6	4/23/81
Down and Out	16	8/28/81
If You're Thinking You Want a Stranger	1	1/7/82
Fool Hearted Memory	1	5/27/82
Marina del Rey	6	9/16/82
Amarillo by Morning	1	1/13/83
A Fire I Can't Put Out	1	5/19/83
You Look So Good in Love	1	9/22/83
Right or Wrong	1	1/25/84
Let's Fall to Pieces Together	1	5/17/84
Does Ft. Worth Ever Cross Your Mind	1	9/4/84
The Cowboy Rides Again	5	1/14/85
The Fireman	5	5/6/85
The Chair	1	8/26/85
You're Something Special to Me	4	12/23/85
Nobody in His Right Mind Would Have Left Her	1	4/21/86
It Ain't Cool to Be Crazy About You	1	8/25/86
Ocean Front Property	1	12/22/86
All My Ex's Live in Texas	1	4/6/87
Am I Blue	1	8/3/87
Famous Last Words of a Fool	1	1/11/88
Baby Blue	1	4/25/88
If You Ain't Lovin' (You Ain't Livin')	1	8/22/88
Baby's Gotten Good at Goodbye	1	12/26/88
What's Going on in Your World	1	4/3/89
Ace in the Hole	1	7/17/89
Overnight Success	8	11/6/89
Love Without End, Amen	1 (5 weeks)	4/6/90
Drinking Champagne	4	7/20/90
I've Come to Expect It from You	1 (5 weeks)	10/22/90
If I Know Me	1 (2 weeks)	3/12/91
You Know Me Better than That	1	6/11/91
Chill of an Early Fall	1	9/23/91
Love Sick Blues	20	1/7/92
Gone As a Girl Can Get	5	4/6/92
So Much Like My Dad	1	6/29/92
I Cross My Heart	1 (2 weeks)	9/14/92
Heartland	1	1/11/93
When Did You Stop Loving Me	1	4/19/93
Easy Come, Easy Go	1	8/9/93
I'd Like to Have That One Back	1	11/22/93
Lovebug	6	2/24/94
The Man in Love with You	2	6/14/94
The Big One	1	9/19/94
You Can't Make a Heart Love Somebody	1	12/5/94
Adalida	2	3/21/95
Lead On	1	6/13/95
Check Yes or No[1]	1 (4 weeks)	9/18/95
I Know She Still Loves Me	1	12/11/95
Blue Clear Sky	1	3/26/96
Carried Away	1 (3 weeks)	6/17/96
I Can Still Make Cheyenne	1	9/2/96
King of the Mountain	12	12/9/96
One Night at a Time	1	3/3/97

1. ACADEMY OF COUNTRY MUSIC AND CMA SINGLE OF THE YEAR

Ace in the Hole

Registration 7
Rhythm: Country or March

Words and Music by
Dennis R. Adkins

8

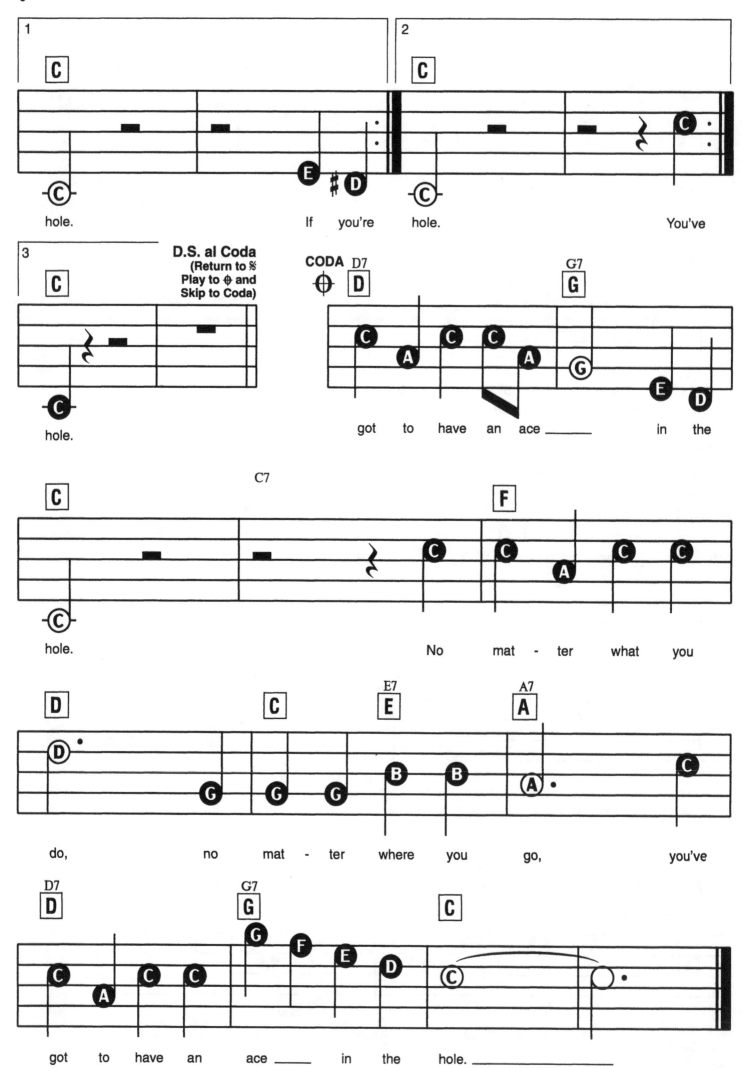

Adalida

Registration 9
Rhythm: Country or Swing

Words and Music by Mike Geiger,
Woody Mullis and Michael Huffman

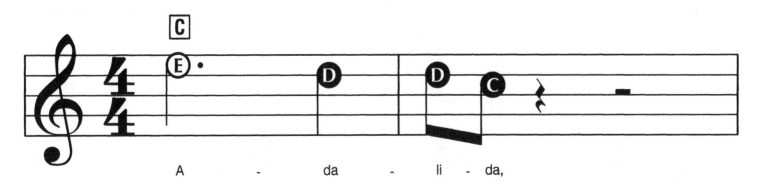

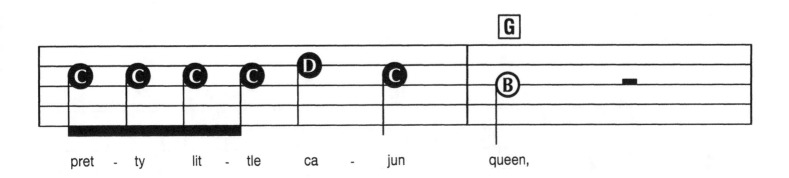

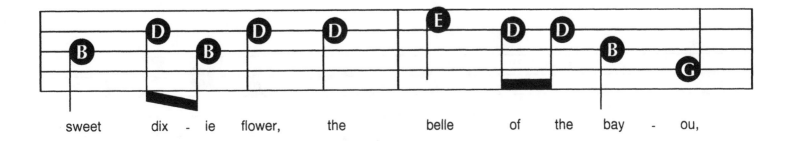

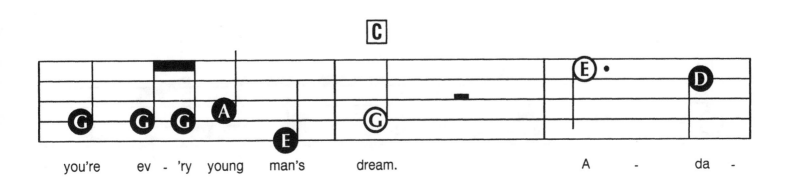

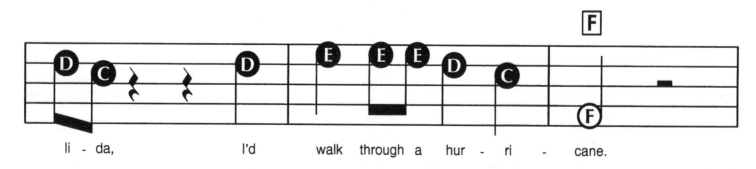

li - da,   I'd   walk through a   hur - ri - cane.

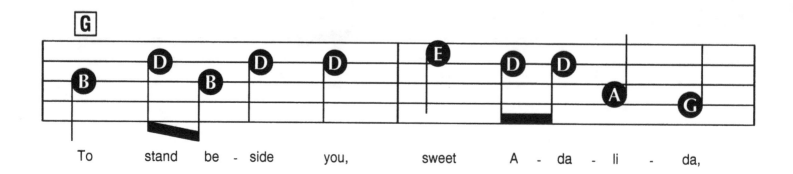

To   stand be - side   you,   sweet A - da - li - da,

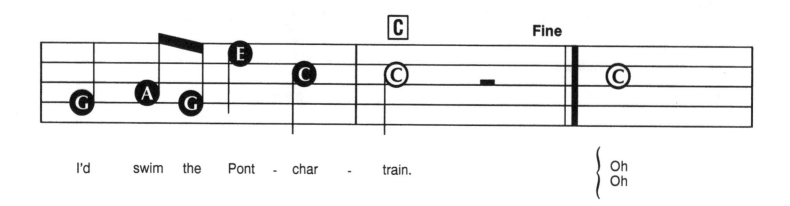

I'd   swim   the   Pont - char - train.

Oh
Oh

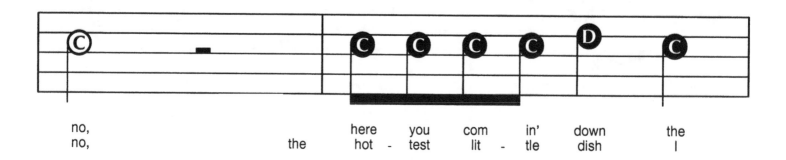

no,   here   you   com   in'   down   the
no,   the   hot - test lit - tle   dish   I

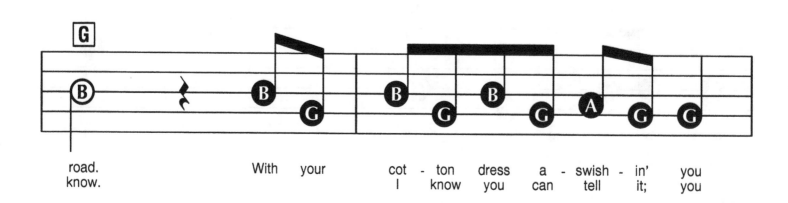

road.   With   your   cot - ton dress a - swish - in'   you
know.   I   know   you   can   tell   it;   you

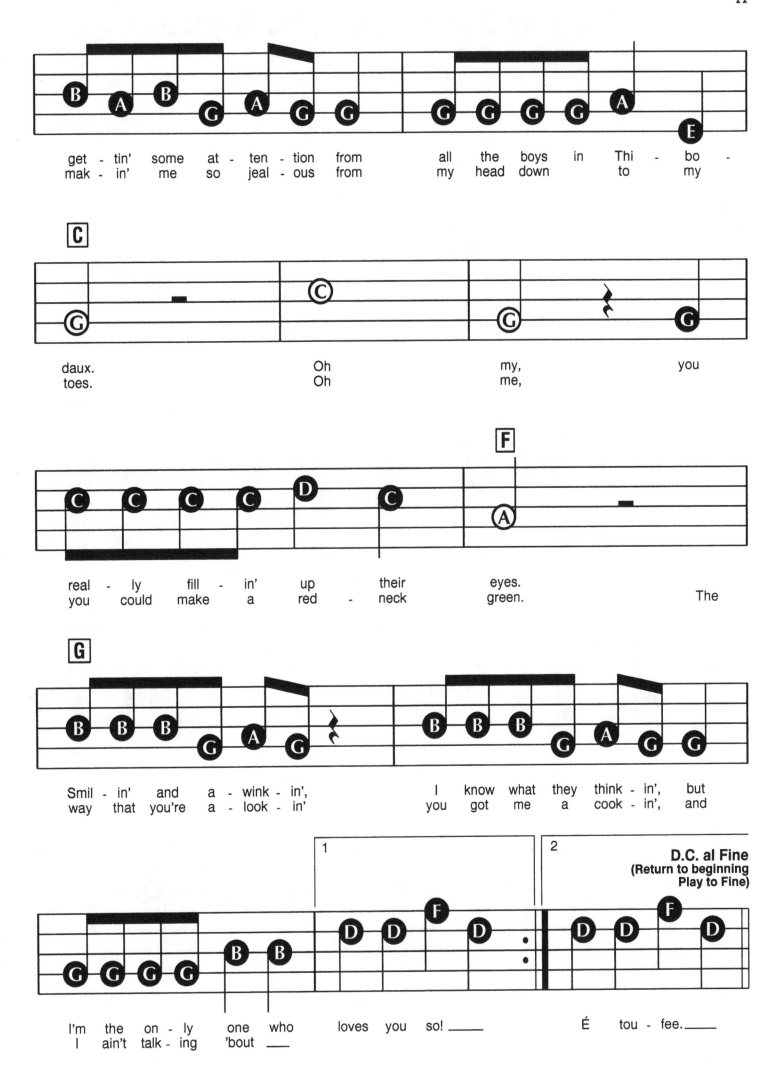

All My Ex's Live in Texas

Registration 4
Rhythm: Country or Shuffle

Words and Music by Sanger D. Shafer
and Linda J. Shafer

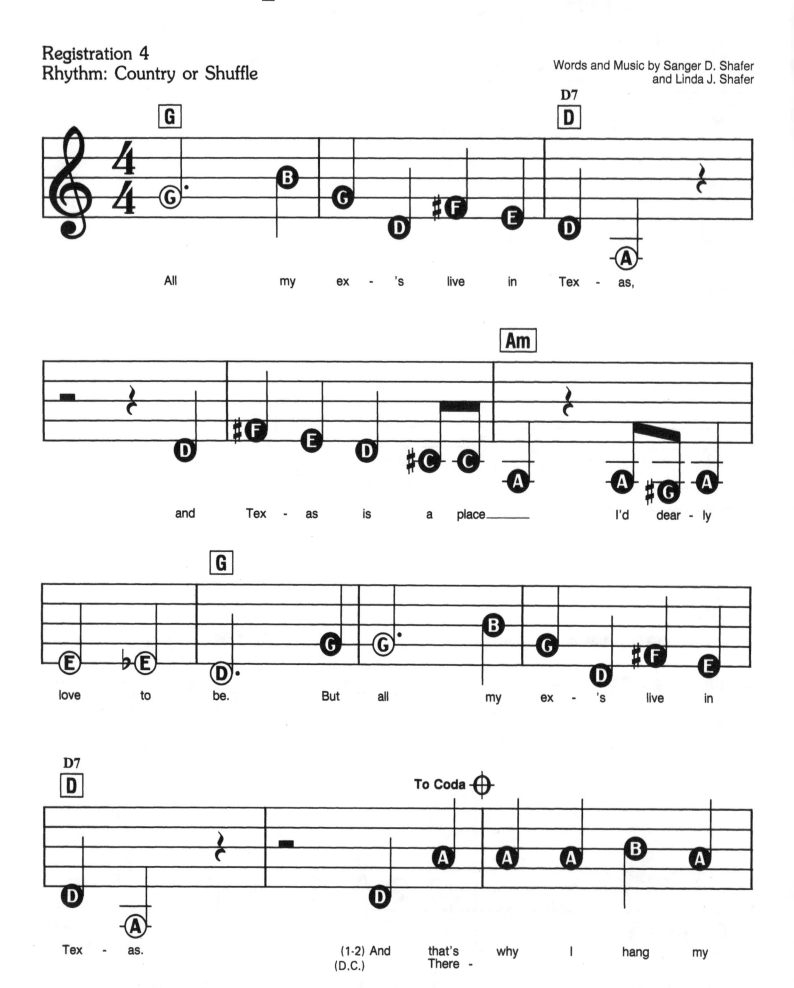

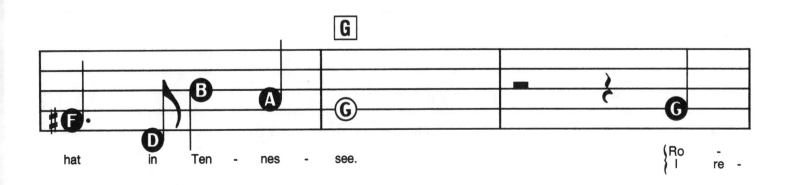

hat   in   Ten - nes - see.   {Ro -
                                                         {I   re -

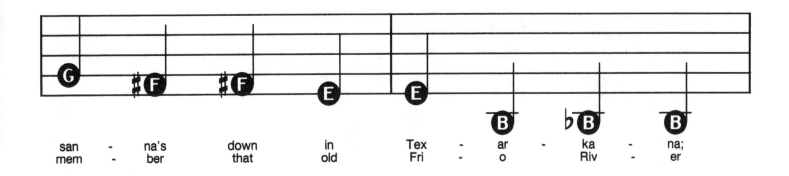

san - na's   down   in   Tex - ar - ka - na;
mem - ber that   old   Fri - o   Riv - er

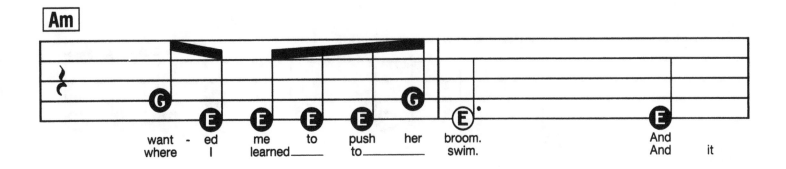

want - ed me to push her broom.   And   it
where I learned to swim.   And   it

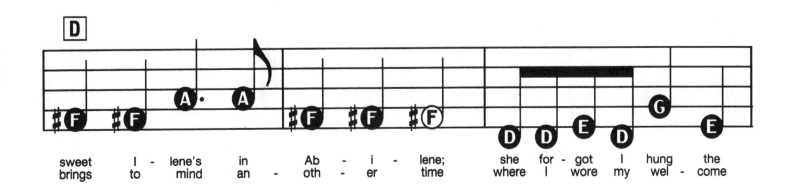

sweet I - lene's in Ab - i - lene; she for - got I hung the
brings to mind an - oth - er time where I wore my wel - come

13

14

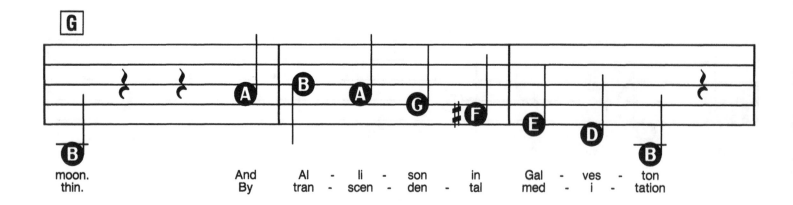

moon. | And | Al - li - son | in | Gal - ves - ton
thin. | By | tran - scen - den - tal | med - i - tation

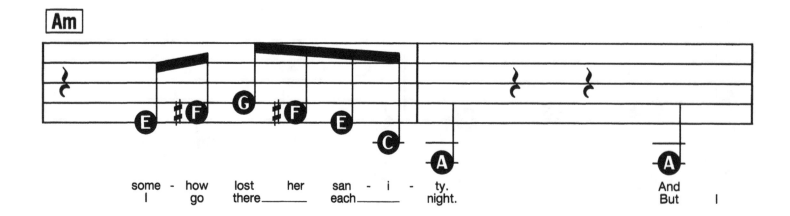

some - how lost her san - i - ty. | And
I go there___ each___ night. | But I

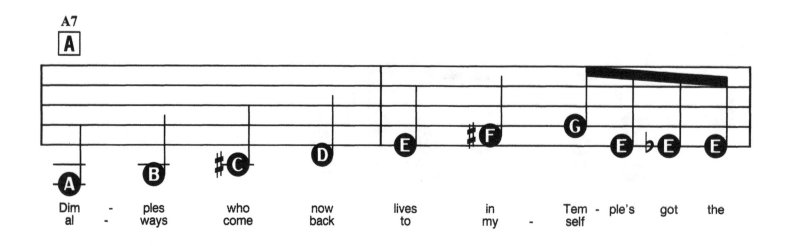

Dim - ples who now lives in Tem - ple's got the
al - ways come back to my - self

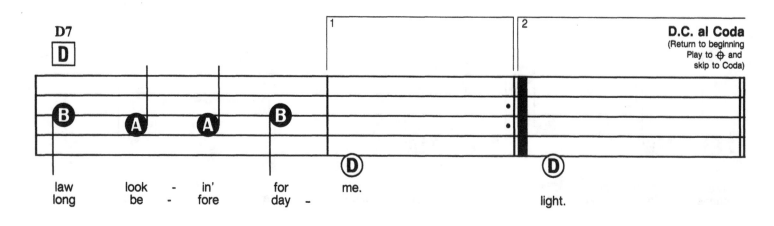

law look - in' for me.
long be - fore day - light.

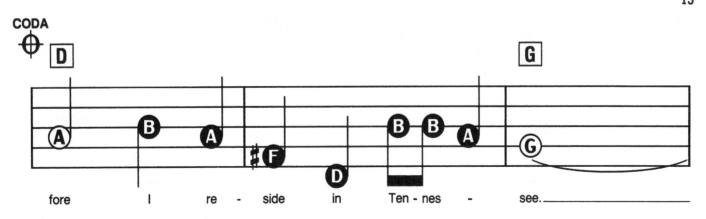

fore I re - side in Ten - nes - see._____

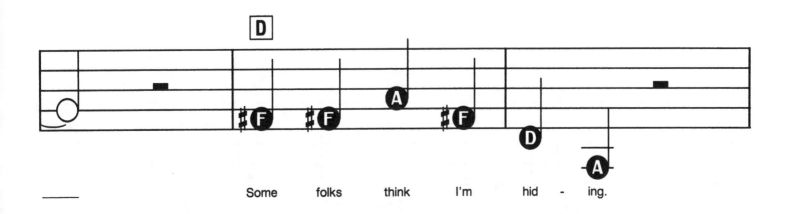

_____ Some folks think I'm hid - ing.

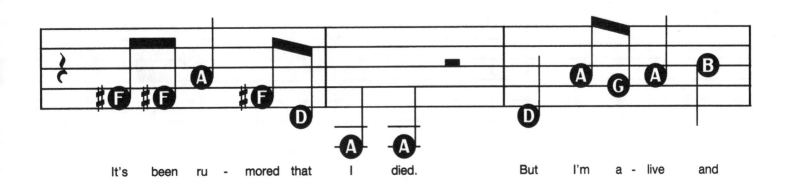

It's been ru - mored that I died. But I'm a - live and

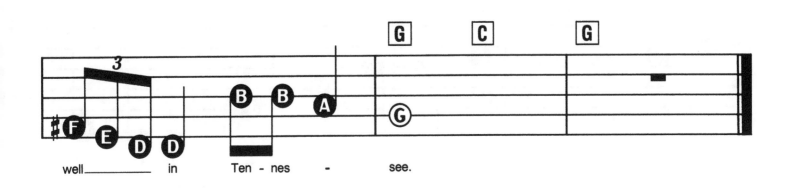

well_____ in Ten - nes - see.

Am I Blue

Registration 2
Rhythm: Pops or 8-Beat

Words and Music by David Chamberlain
and George Strait

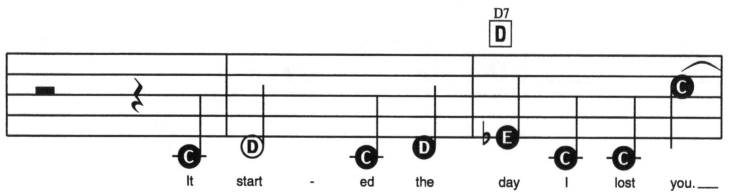

Am   I   blue? _____   Yes, I'm _____ blue.

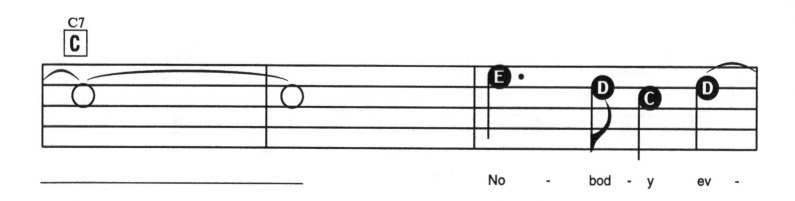

It start - ed the   day   I   lost you. ___

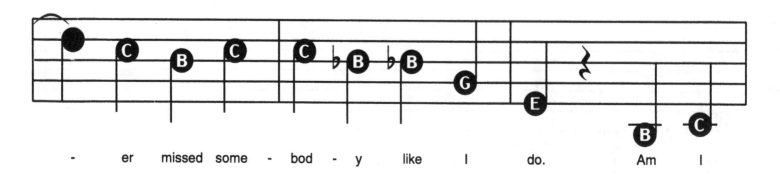

No - bod - y ev -

- er missed some - bod - y like I do.   Am   I

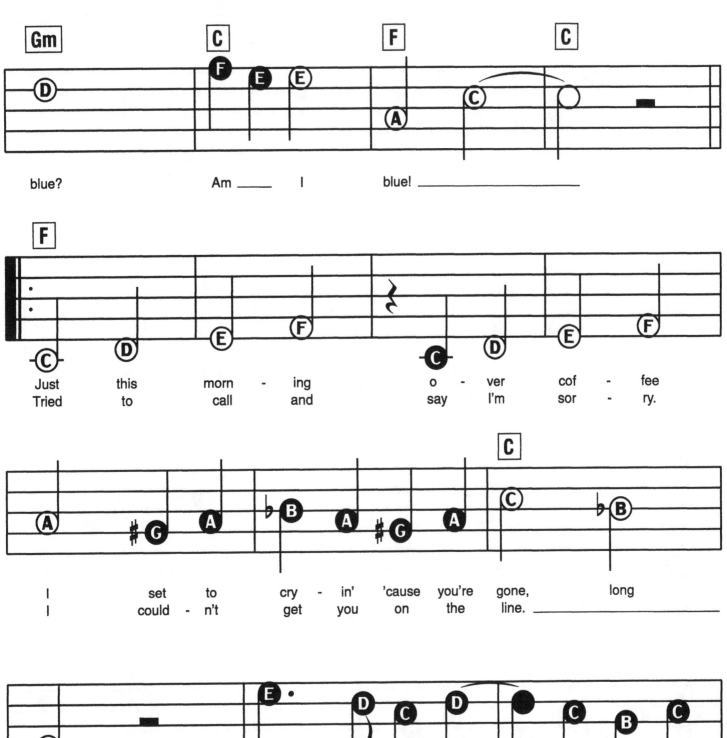

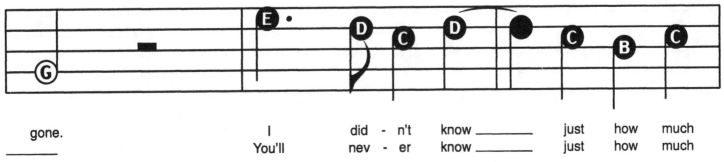

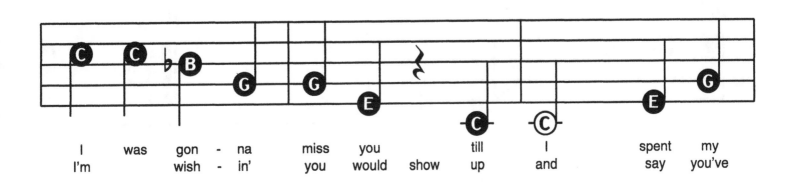

18

Baby Blue

Registration 7
Rhythm: Ballad or Country

Words and Music by
Aaron Barker

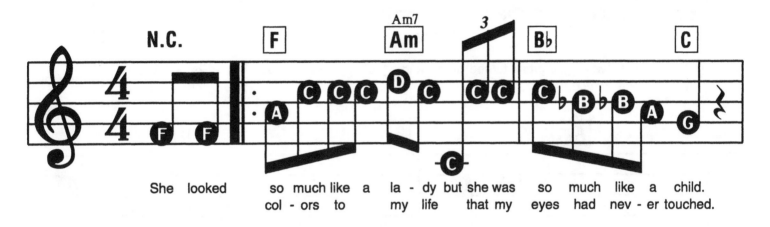

She looked so much like a la - dy but she was so much like a child.
col - ors to my life that my eyes had nev - er touched.

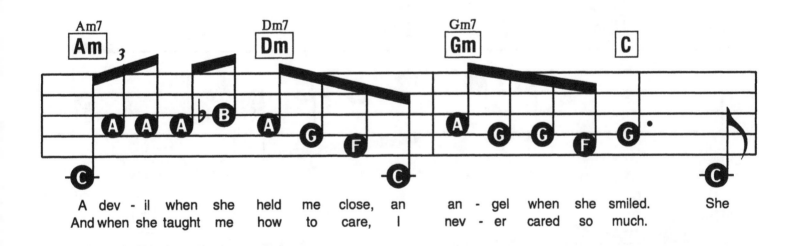

A dev - il when she held me close, an an - gel when she smiled. She
And when she taught me how to care, I nev - er cared so much.

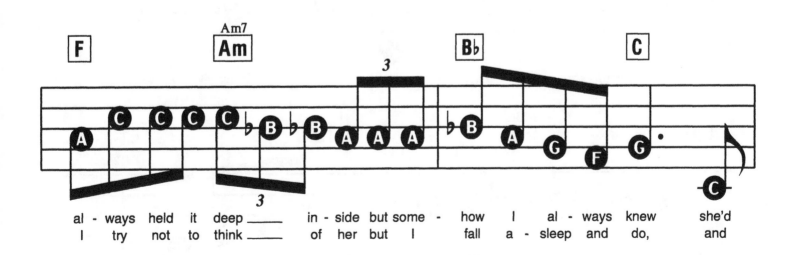

al - ways held it deep _____ in - side but some - how I al - ways knew, she'd
I try not to think _____ of her but I fall a - sleep and do, and

20

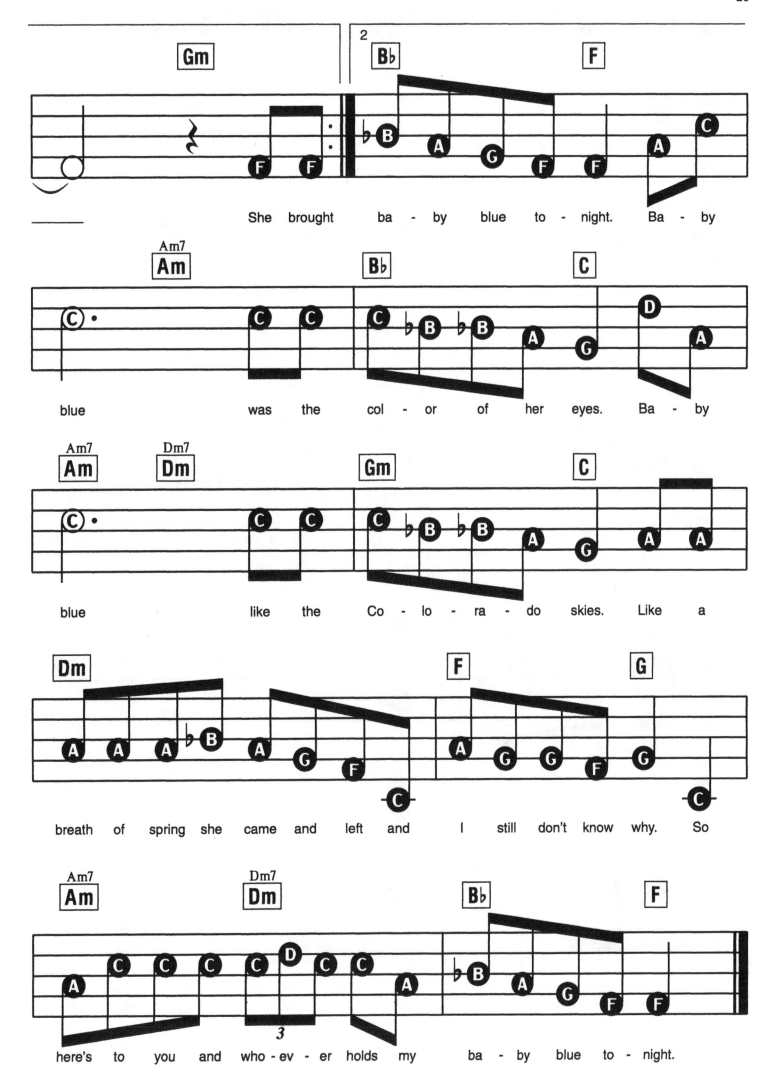

Baby's Gotten Good at Goodbye

Registration 8
Rhythm: 8-Beat or Pops

Words and Music by Tony Martin
and Troy Martin

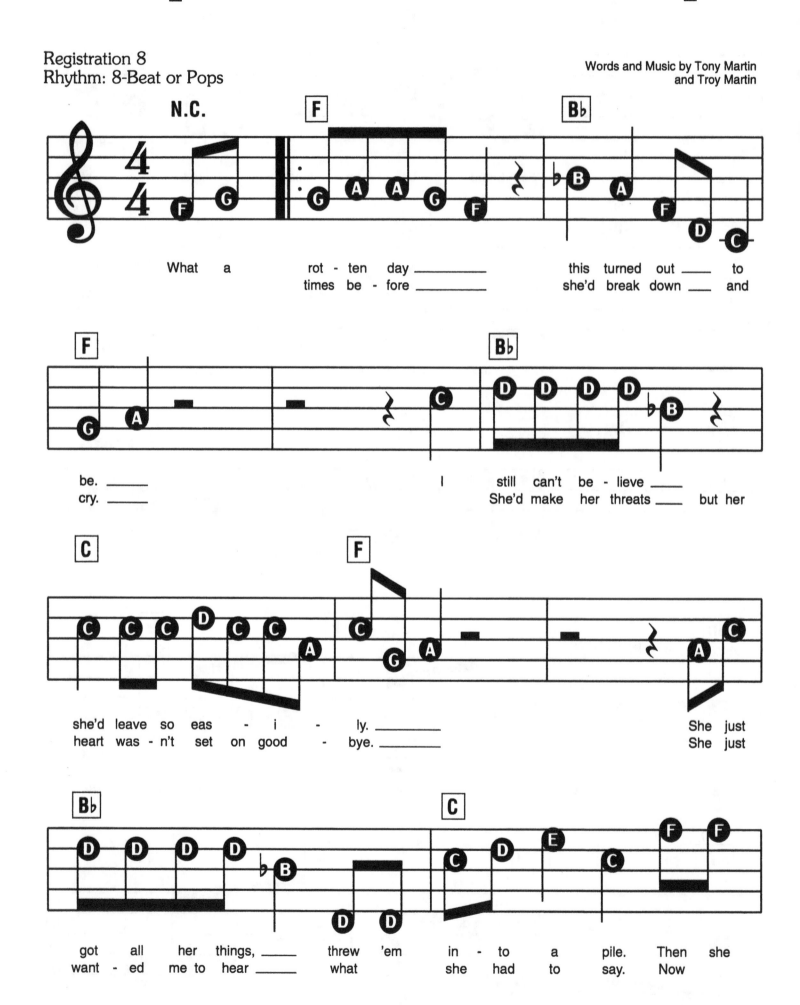

23

The Big One

Registration 10
Rhythm: Shuffle or Swing

Words and Music by Gerry House
and Devon O'Day

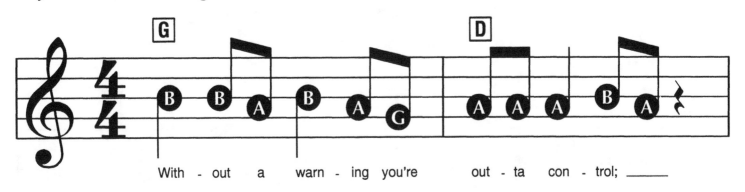

With - out a warn - ing you're out - ta con - trol; _____

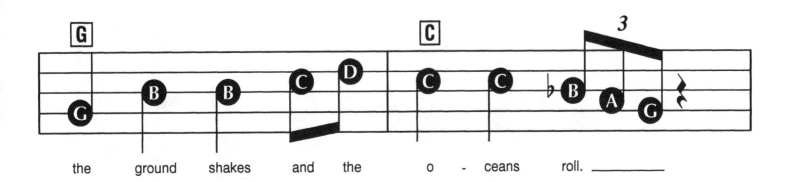

the ground shakes and the o - ceans roll. _____

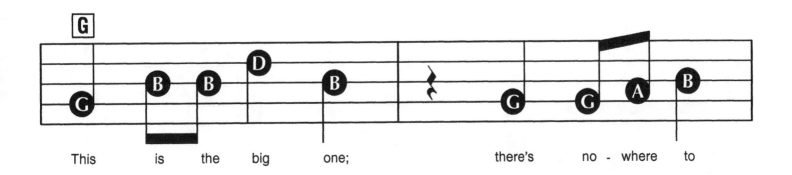

This is the big one; there's no - where to

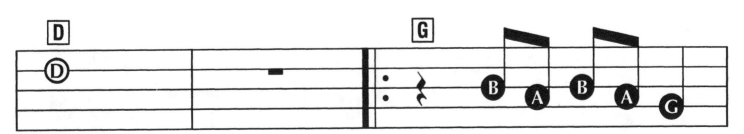

run. On the Rich - ter scale
Instrumental solo

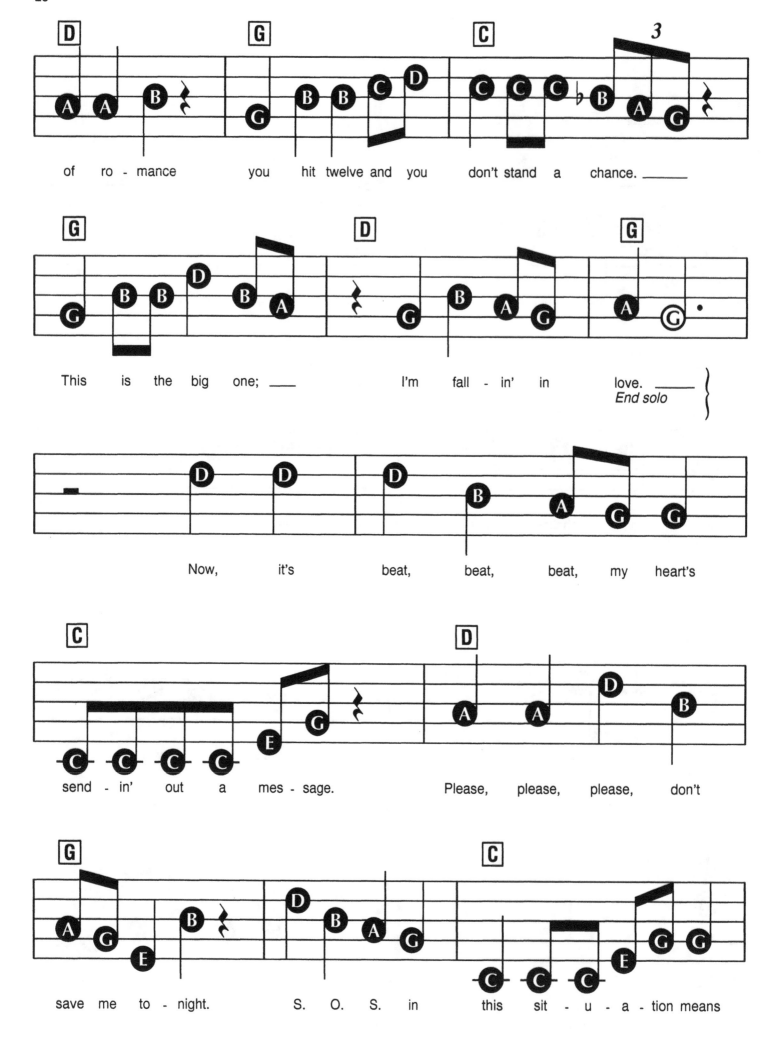

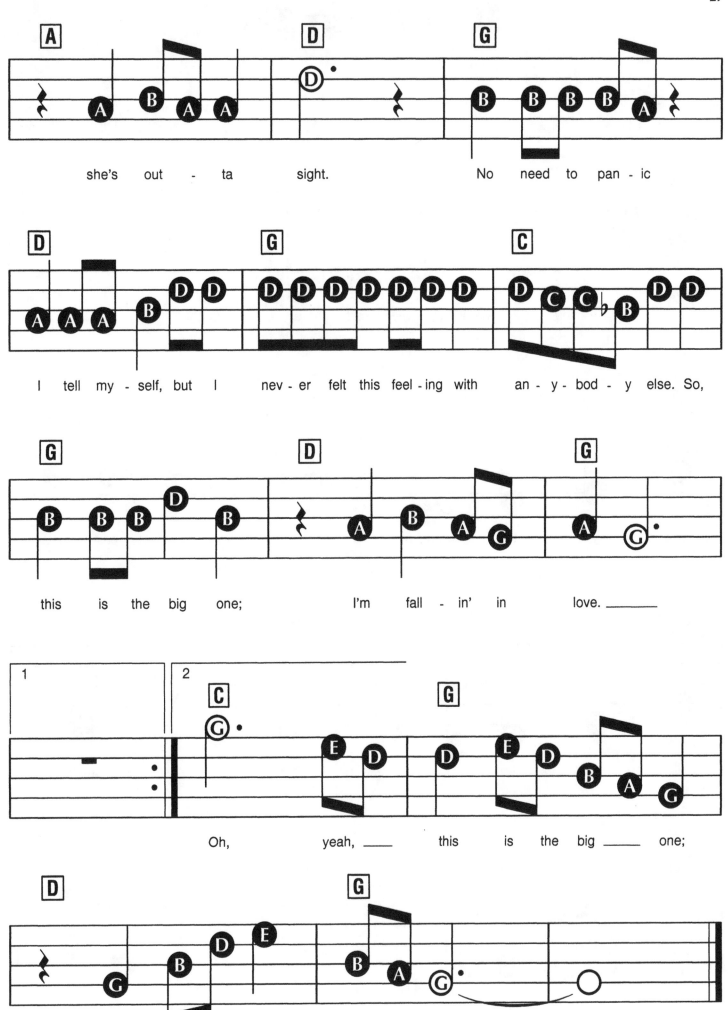

Blue Clear Sky

Registration 2
Rhythm: 8 Beat or Pops

Words and Music by Mark D. Sanders,
Bob DiPiero and John Jarrard

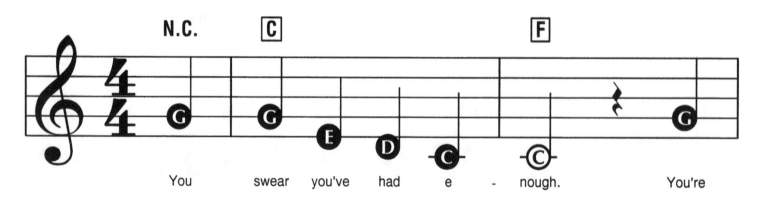

You swear you've had e - nough. You're

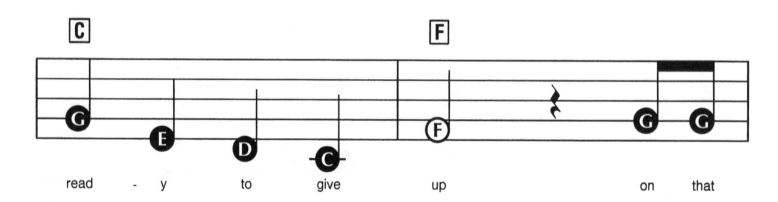

read - y to give up on that

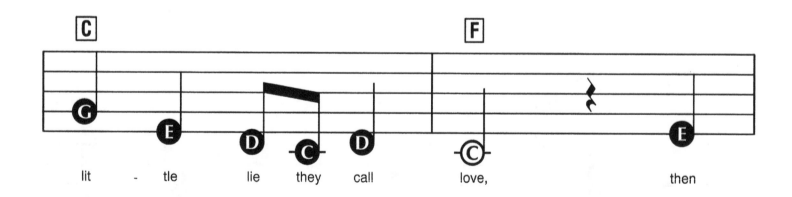

lit - tle lie they call love, then

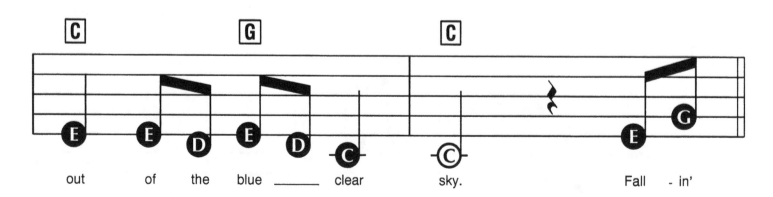

out of the blue _____ clear sky. Fall - in'

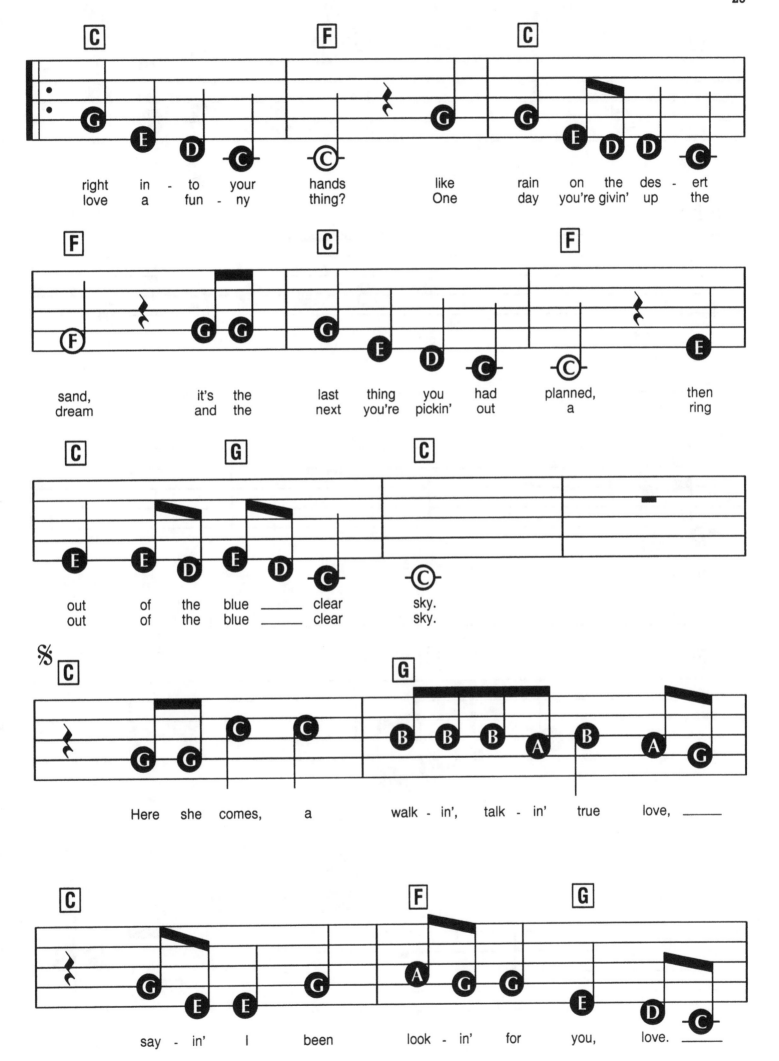

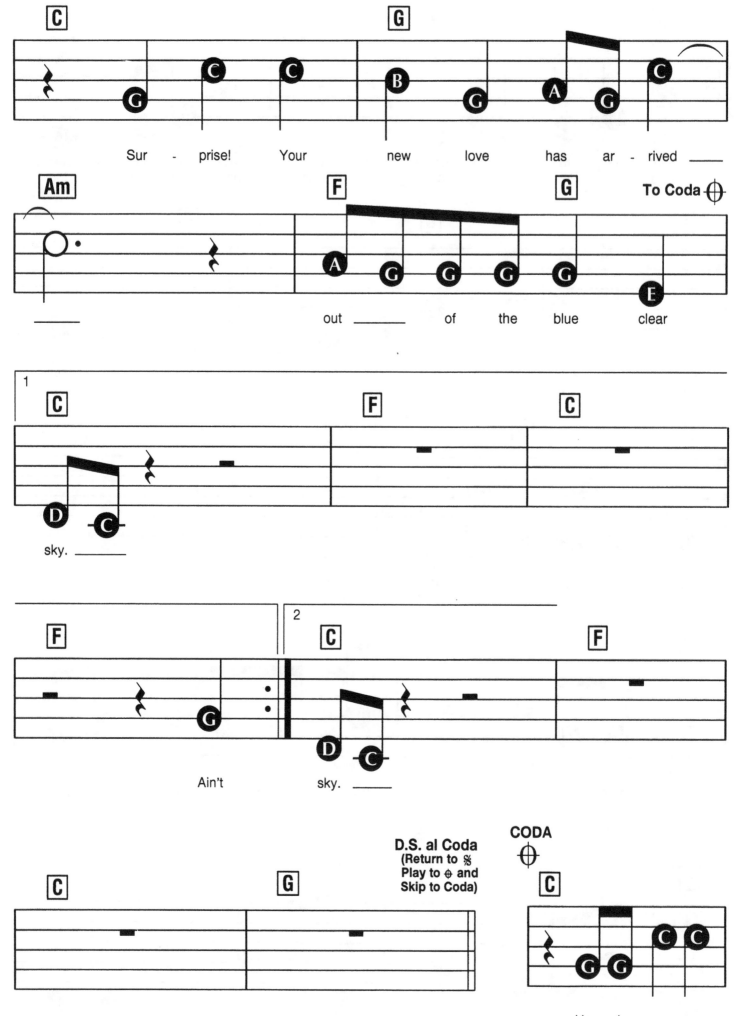

Sur - prise! Your new love has ar - rived ____

____ out ____ of the blue clear

sky. ____

Ain't sky. ____

D.S. al Coda
(Return to %
Play to ⊕ and
Skip to Coda)

CODA
⊕

Here she comes, a

31

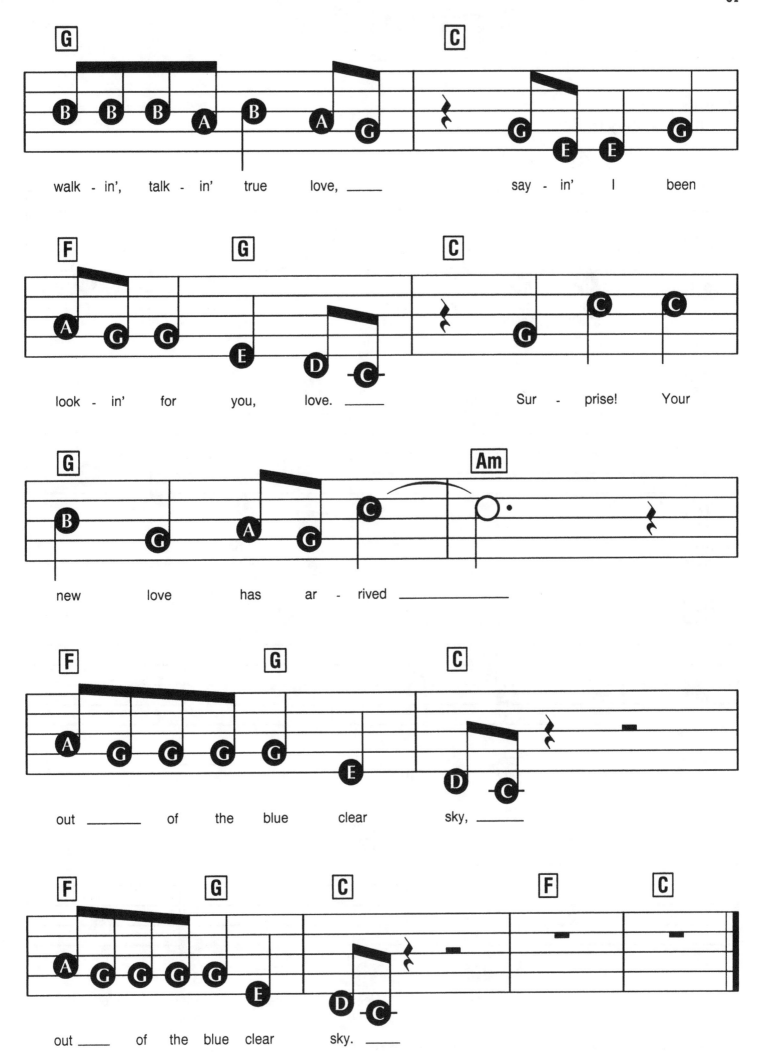

Carried Away

Registration 8
Rhythm: Country or Rock

Words and Music by Steve Bogard
and Jeff Stevens

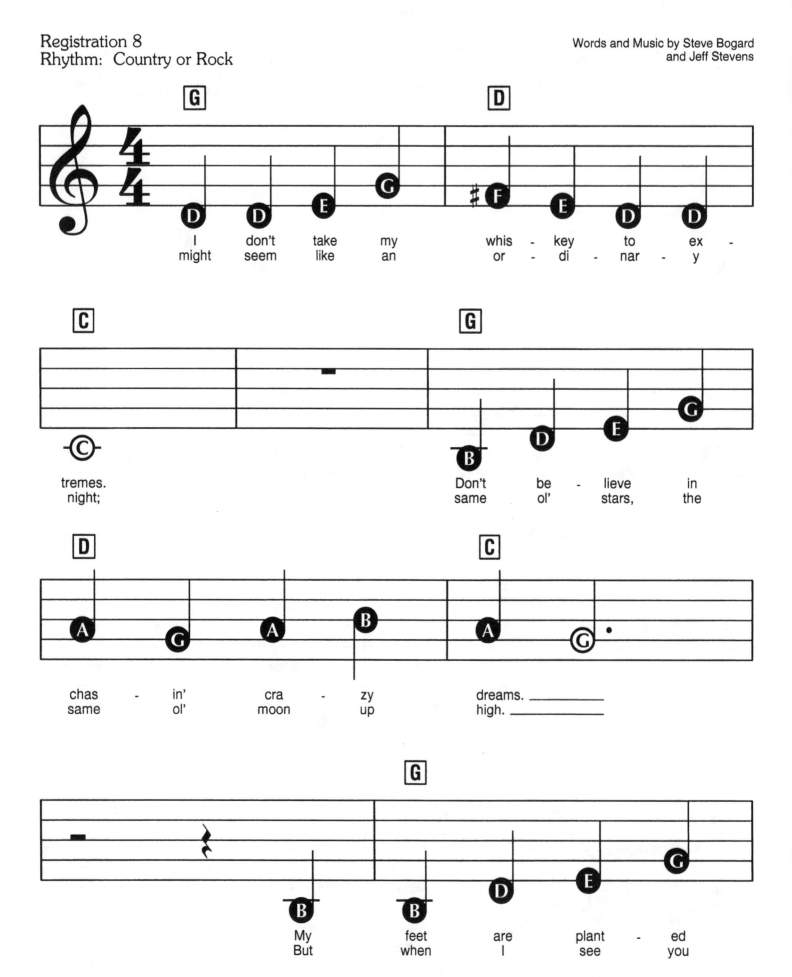

34

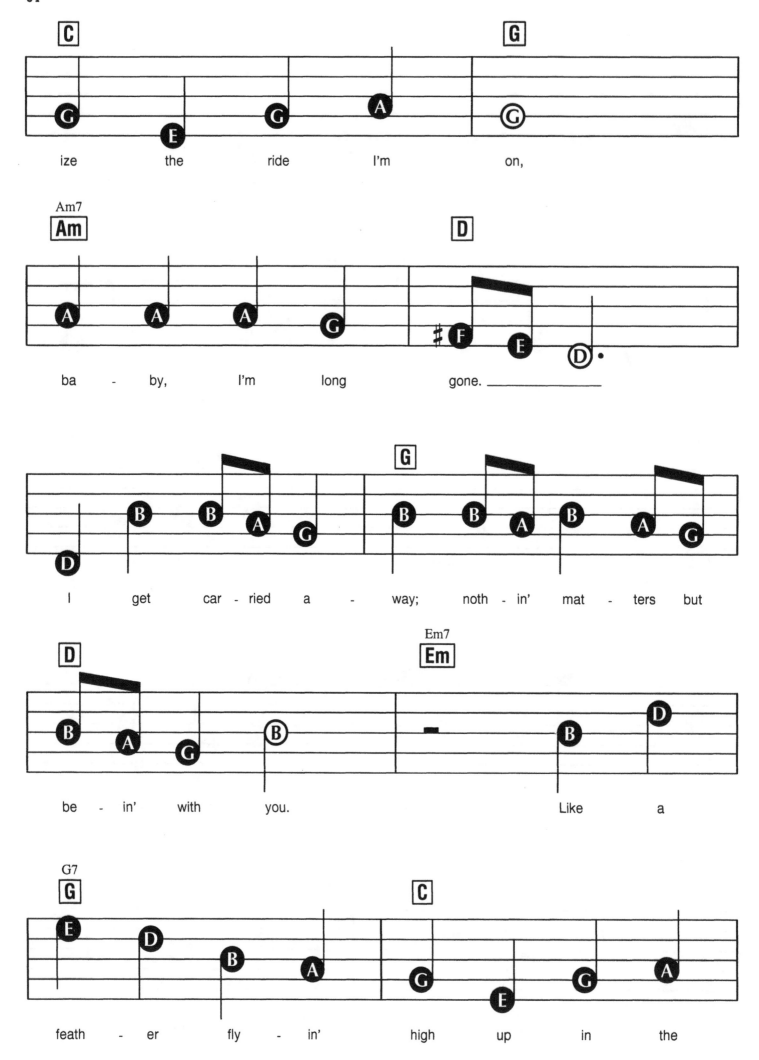

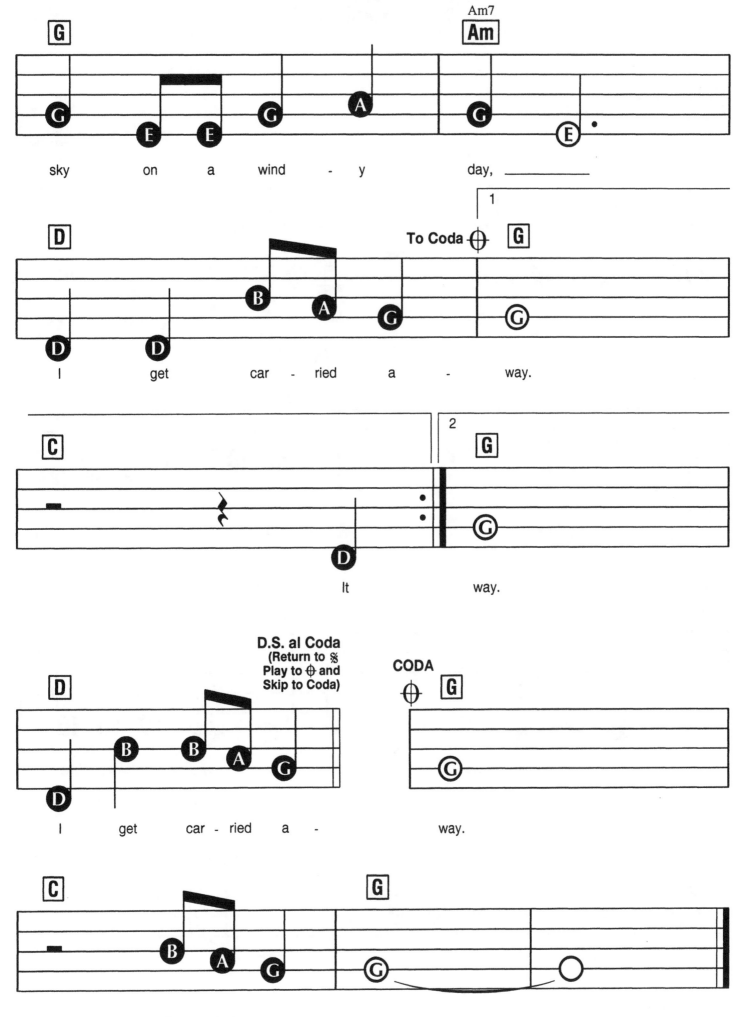

The Chair

Registration 1
Rhythm: Country or Shuffle

Words and Music by Hank Cochran
and Dean Dillon

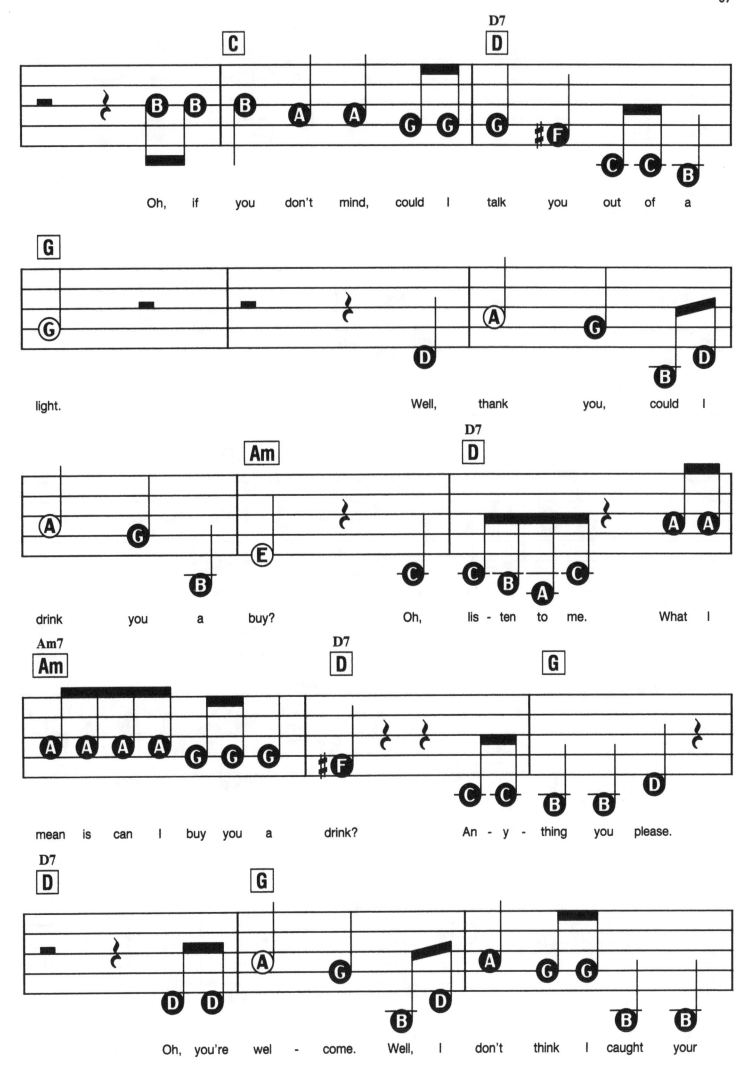

38

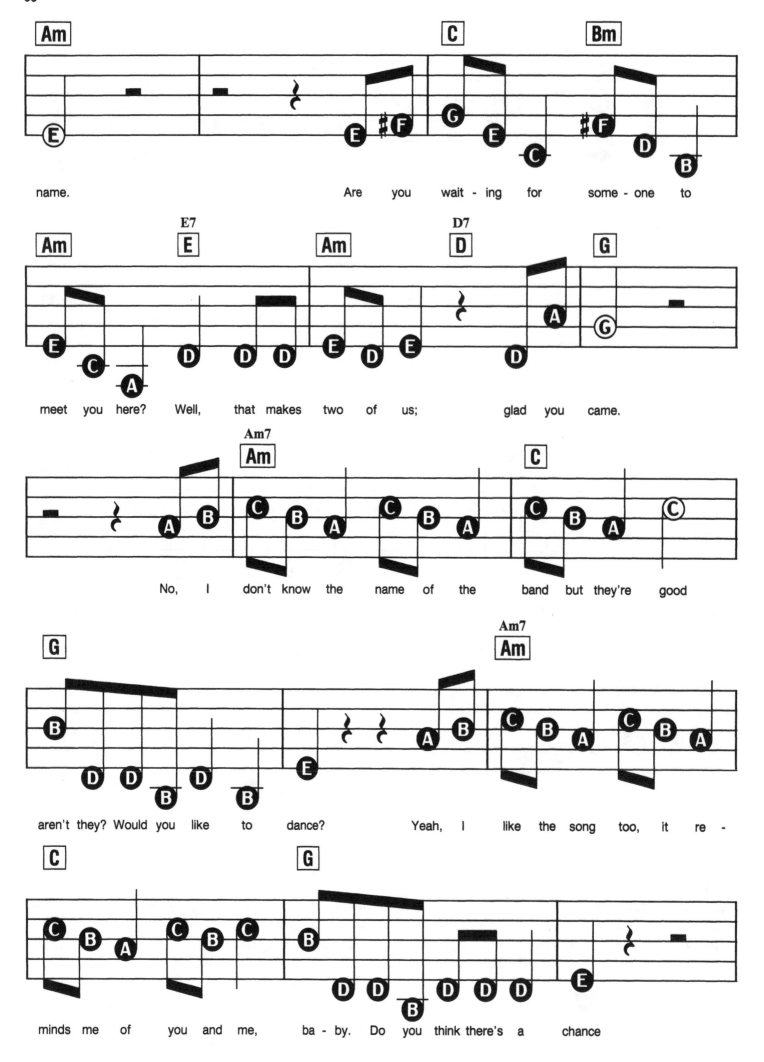

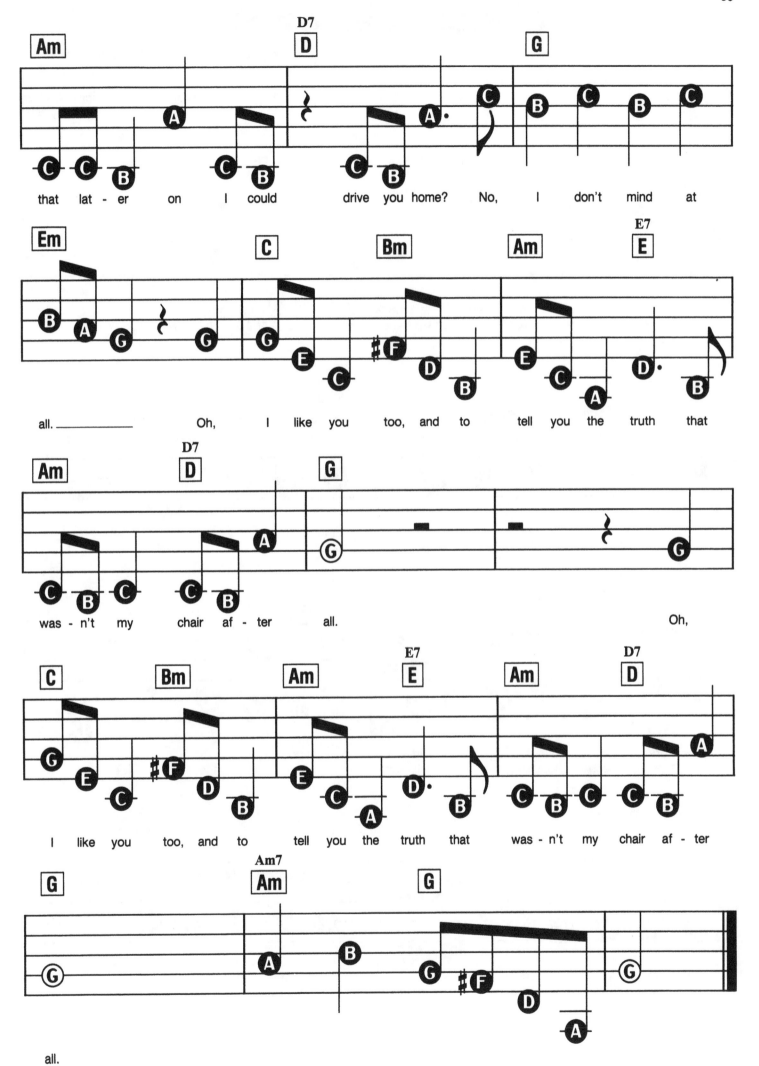

Check Yes or No

Registration 8
Rhythm: Ballad

Words and Music by Danny M. Wells
and Dana H. Oglesby

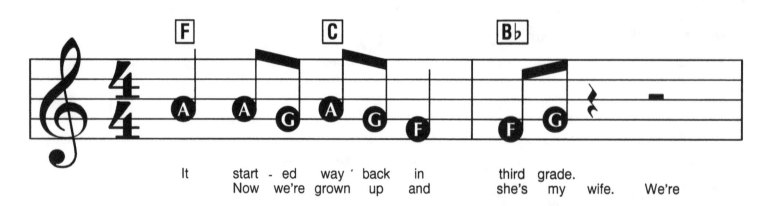

It start - ed way back in third grade.
Now we're grown up and she's my wife. We're

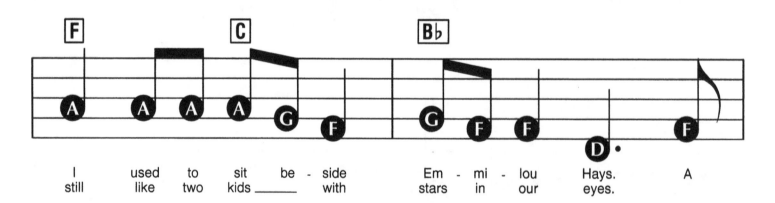

I used to sit be - side Em - mi - lou Hays. A
still like two kids with stars in our eyes.

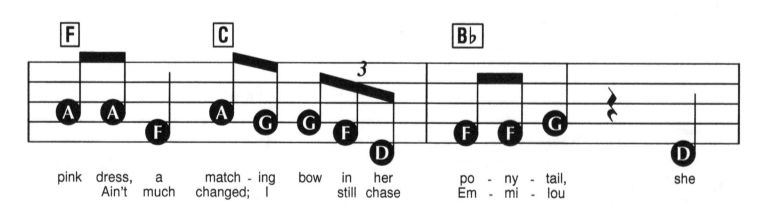

pink dress, a match - ing bow in her po - ny - tail, she
Ain't much changed; I still chase Em - mi - lou

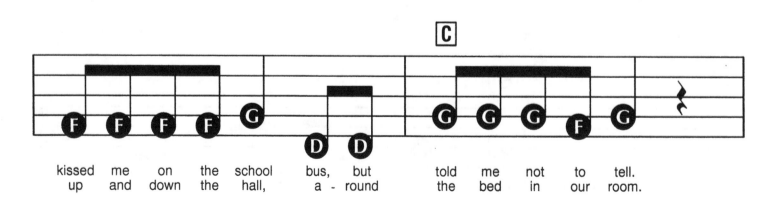

kissed me on the school bus, but told me not to tell.
up and down the hall, a - round the bed in our room.

41

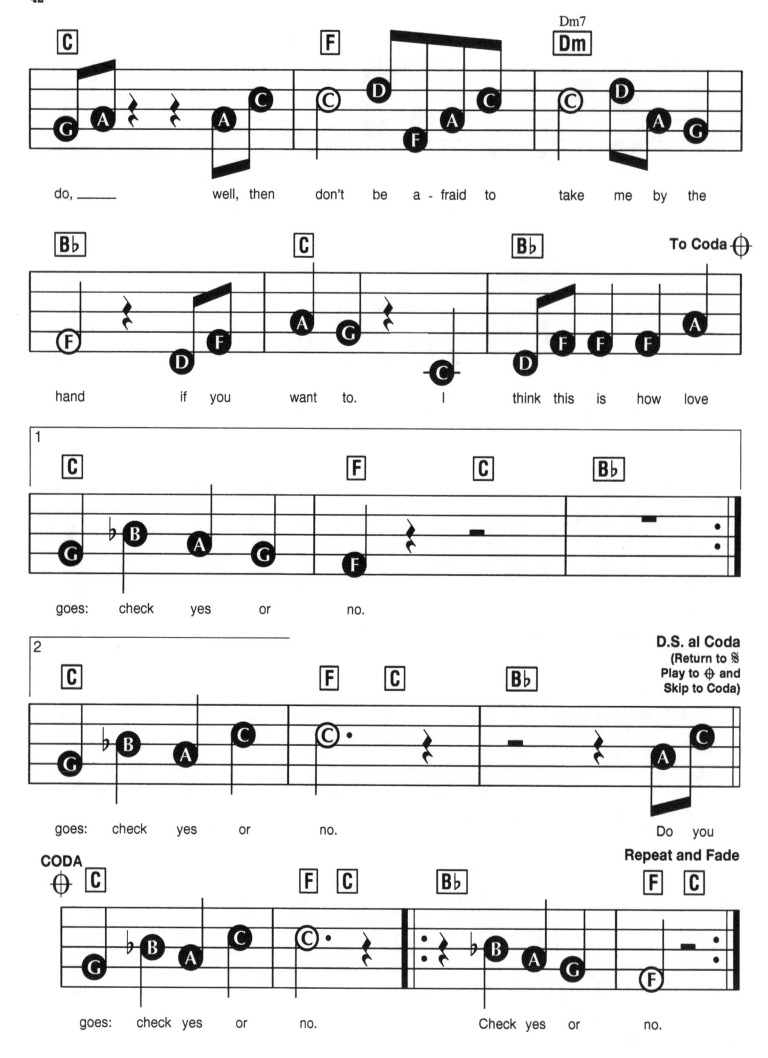

Does Fort Worth Ever Cross Your Mind

Registration 2
Rhythm: Country or Shuffle

Words and Music by Sanger D. Shafer
and Darlene Shafer

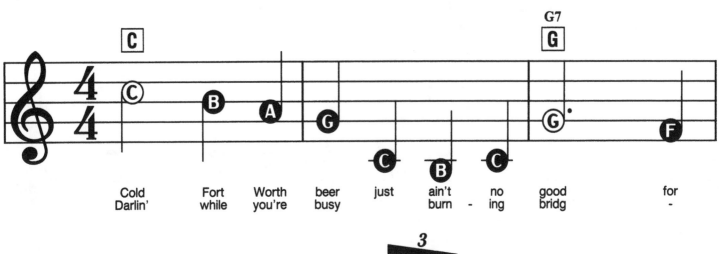

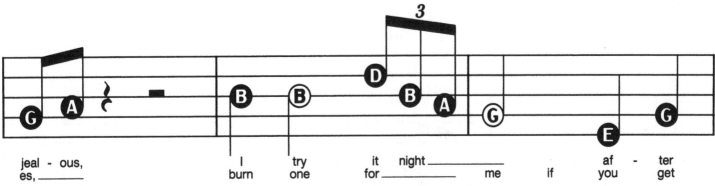

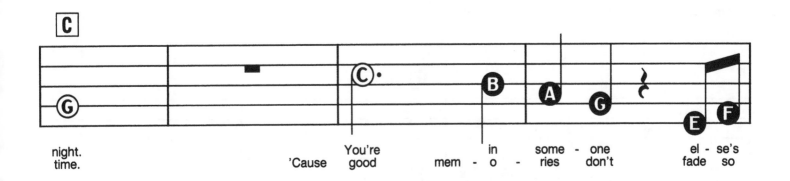

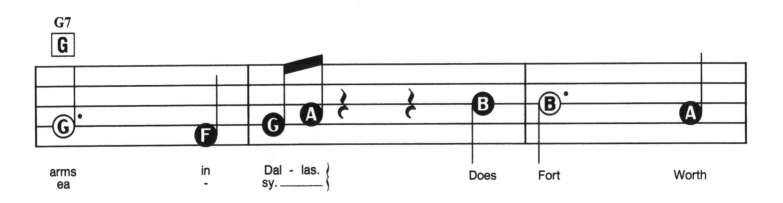

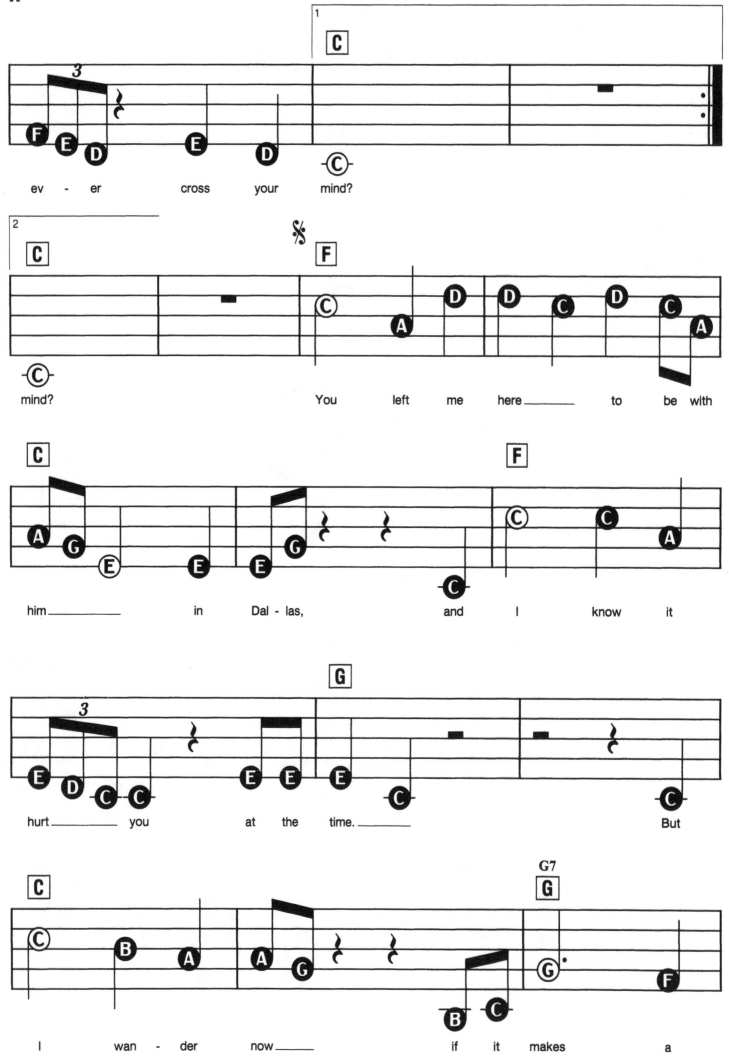

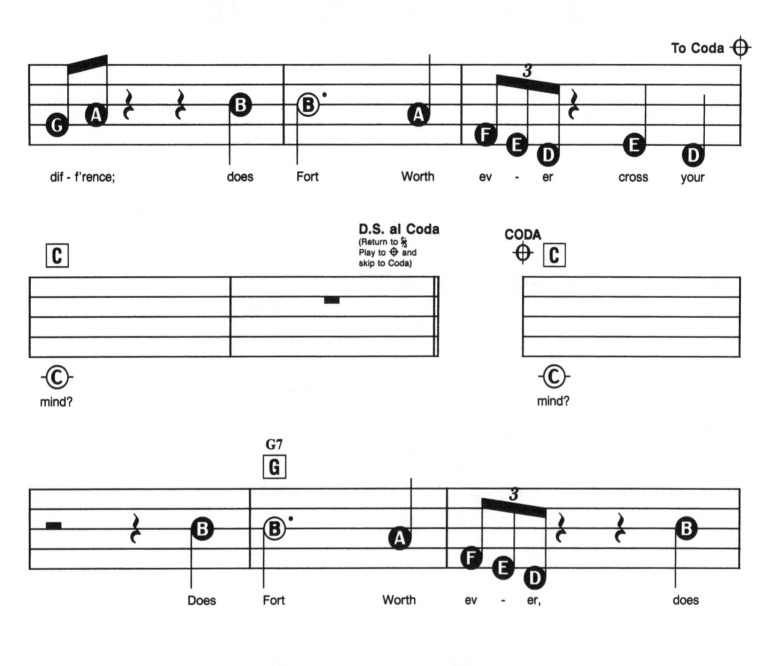

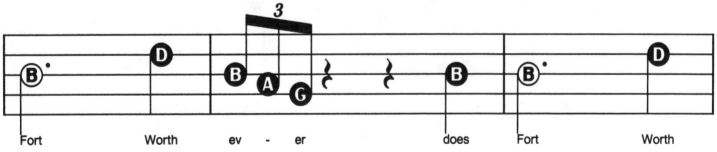

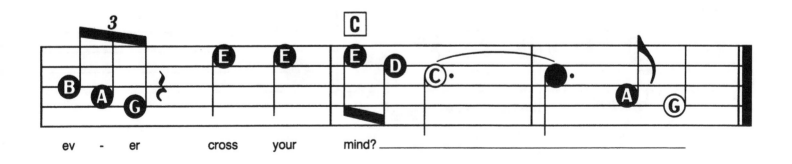

Easy Come, Easy Go

Registration 7
Rhythm: Pop or 8 Beat

Words and Music by Aaron Barker
and Dean Dillon

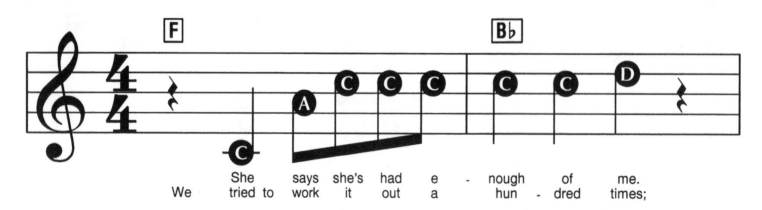

She says she's had e - nough of me.
We tried to work it out a hun - dred times;

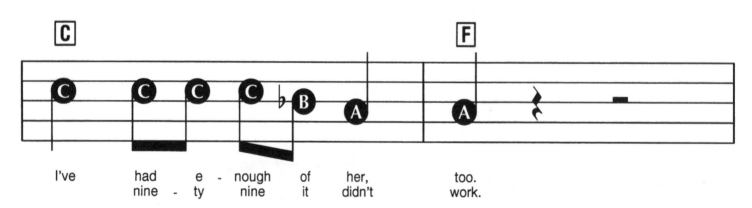

I've had e - nough of her, too.
nine - ty nine it didn't work.

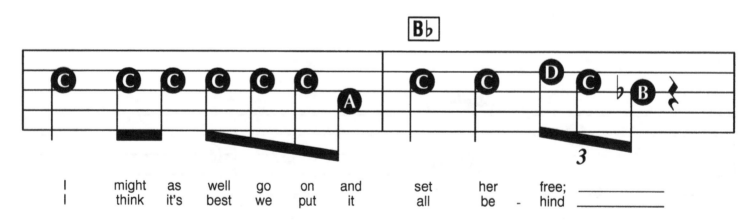

I might as well go on and set her free; _____
I think it's best we put it all be - hind _____

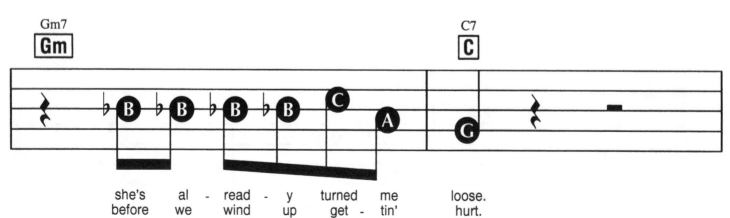

she's al - read - y turned me loose.
before we wind up get - tin' hurt.

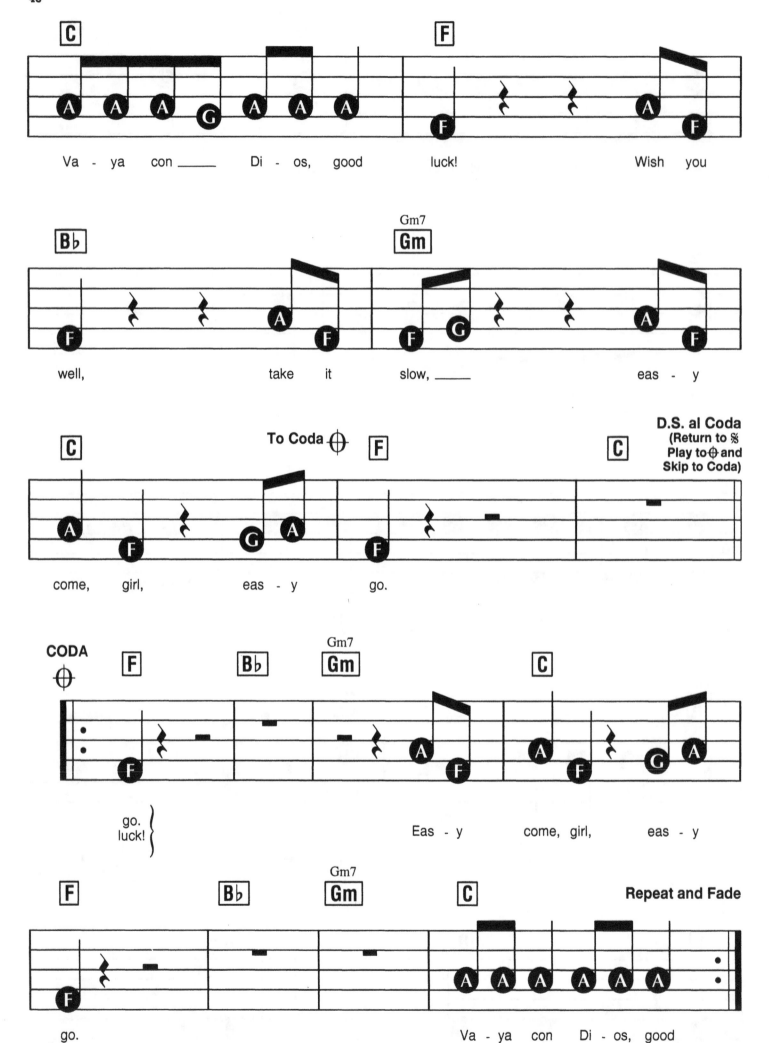

A Fire I Can't Put Out

Registration 2
Rhythm: Country or Shuffle

Words and Music by
Darrel Staedtler

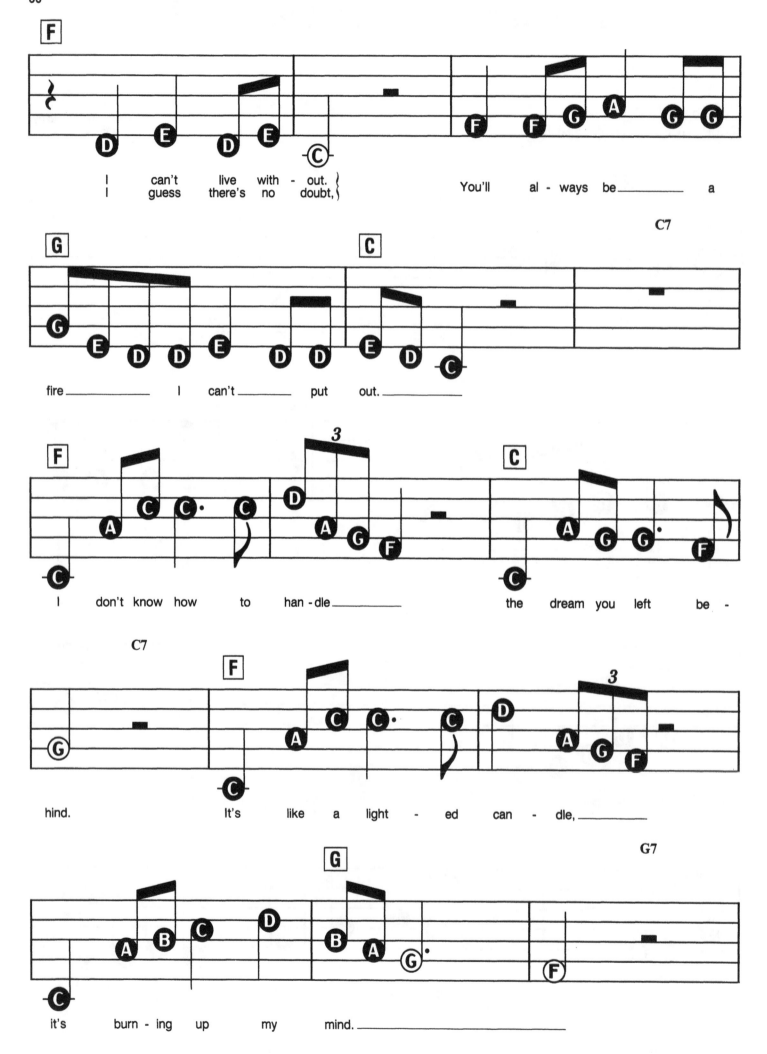

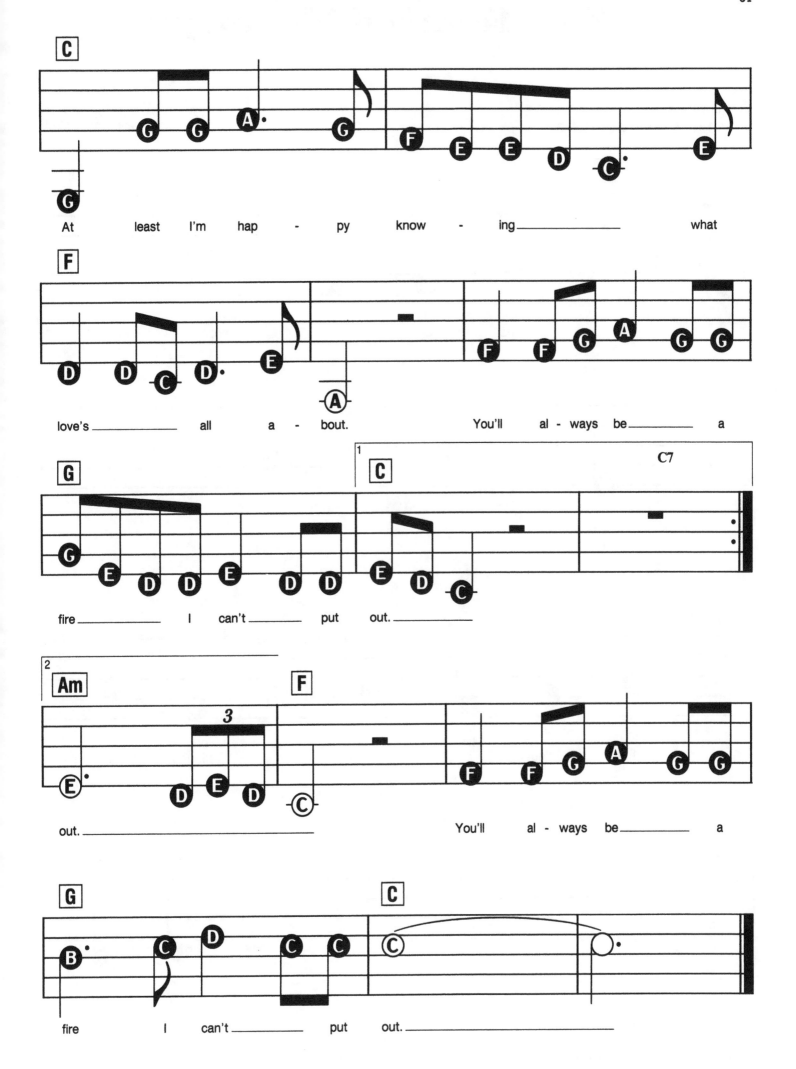

Fool Hearted Memory

Registration 4
Rhythm: Country or Polka

Words and Music by Byron Hill
and Alan R. Mevis

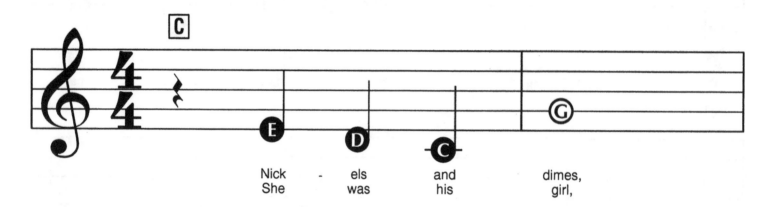

| Nick | - | els | and | his | dimes, |
| She | | was | | his | girl, |

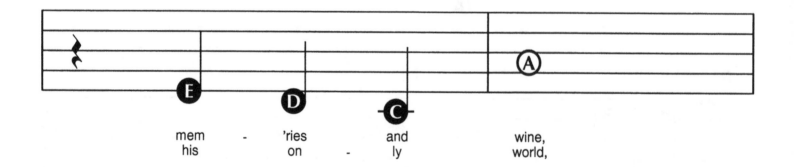

| mem | - | 'ries | and | wine, |
| his | | on | - | ly | world, |

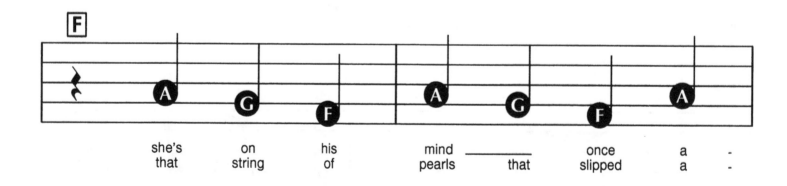

| she's | on | his | mind _____ | once | a - |
| that | string | of | pearls that | slipped | a - |

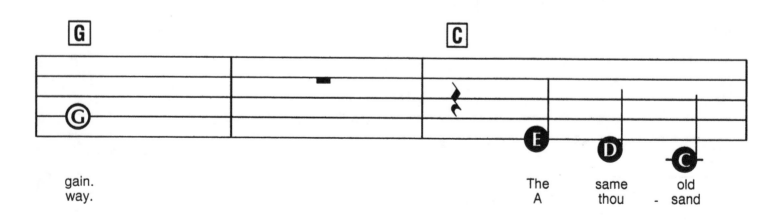

| gain. | | The | same | old |
| way. | | A | thou - | sand |

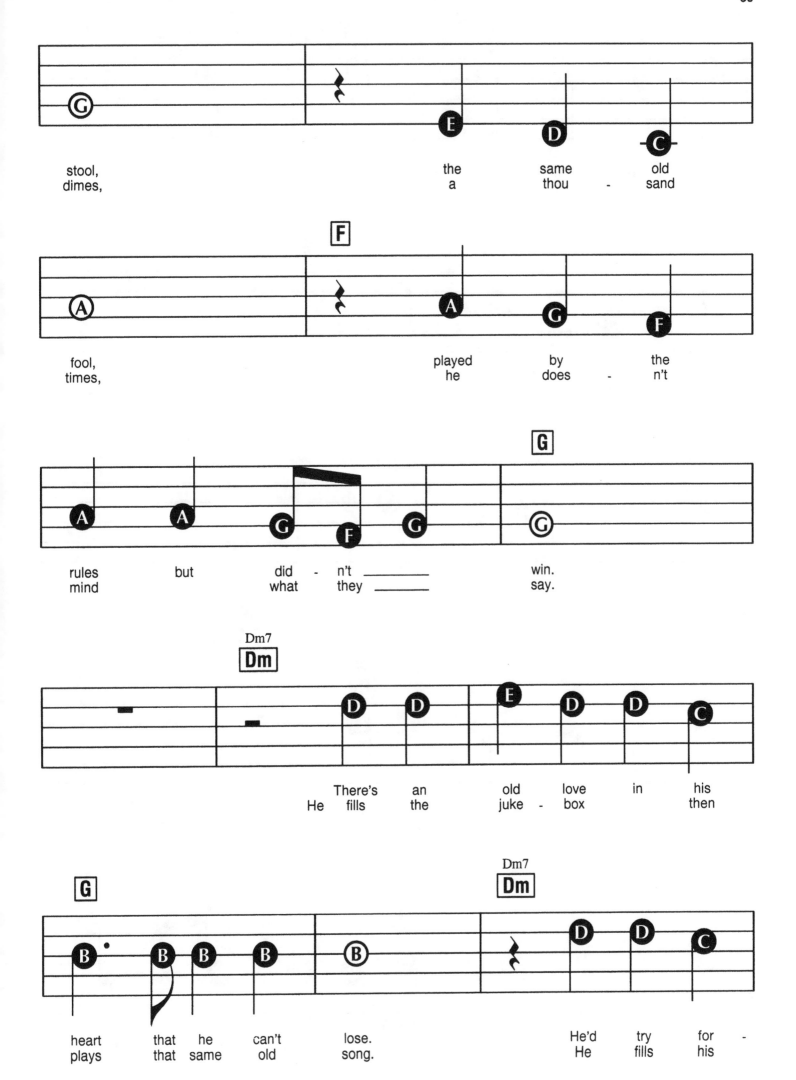

54

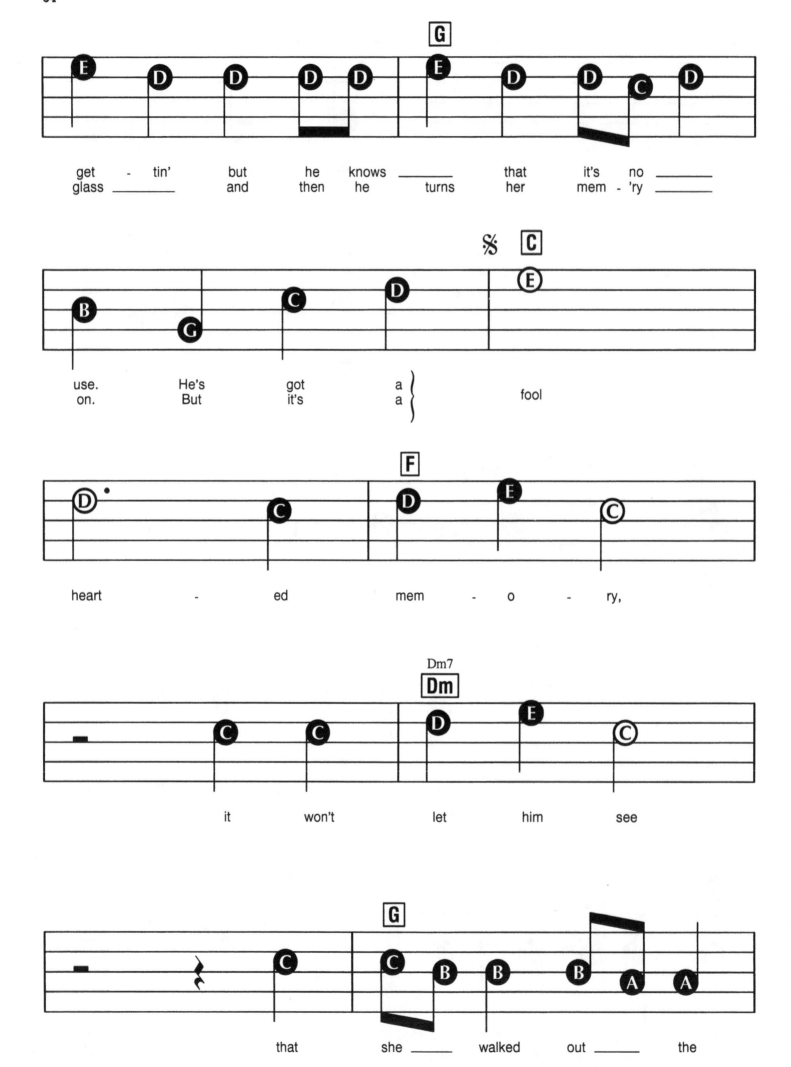

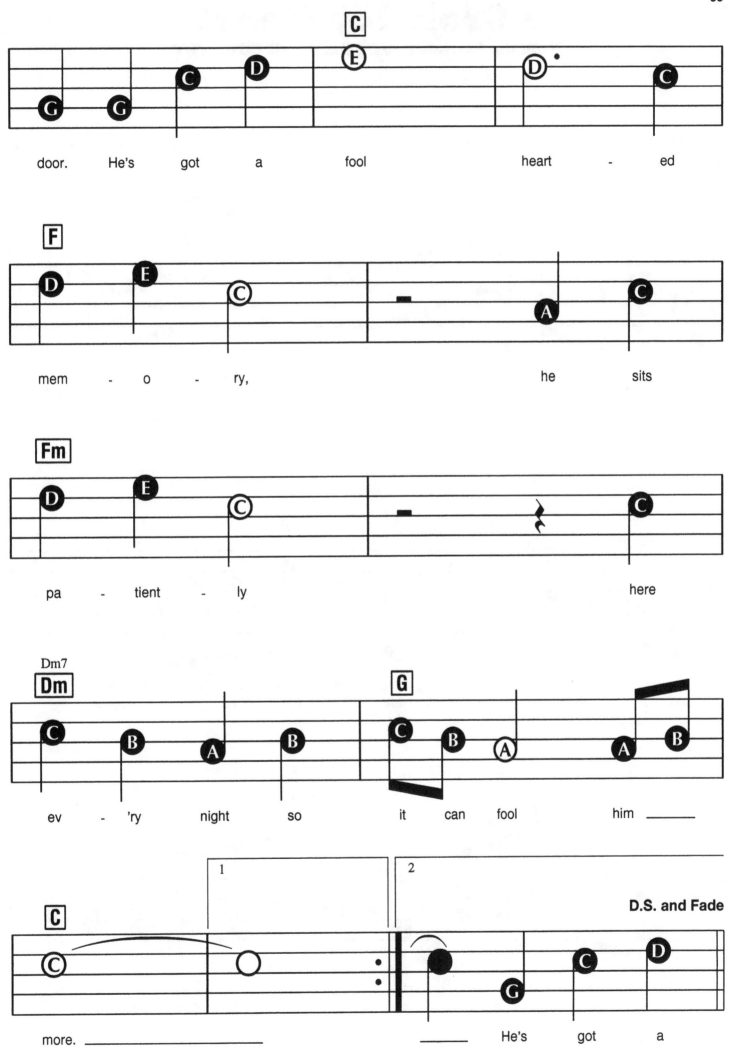

door. He's got a fool heart - ed

mem - o - ry, he sits

pa - tient - ly here

ev - 'ry night so it can fool him _____

D.S. and Fade

more. _____ _____ He's got a

I Cross My Heart
from the Warner Bros. Film PURE COUNTRY

Registration 8
Rhythm: 8-Beat or Pops

Words and Music by Steve Dorff
and Eric Kaz

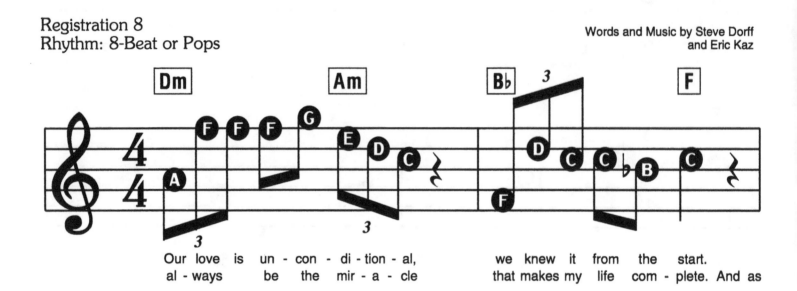

Our love is un - con - di - tion - al,	we knew it from the start.
al - ways	be	the	mir - a - cle	that makes my life com - plete. And as

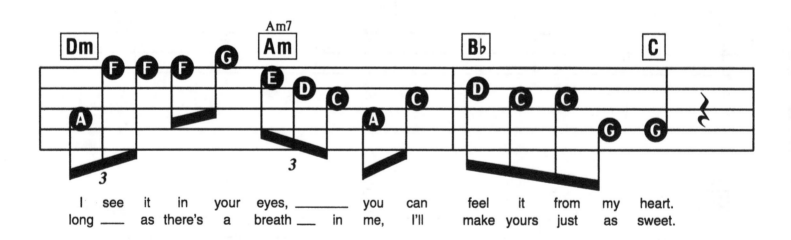

I	see	it	in	your	eyes, _____	you	can	feel	it	from	my	heart.
long ____	as	there's	a	breath ____	in	me,	I'll	make	yours	just	as	sweet.

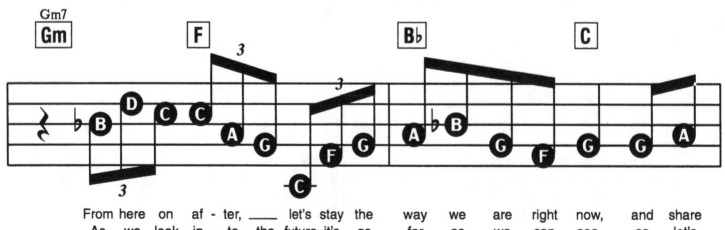

From	here	on	af - ter, ____	let's	stay	the	way	we	are	right	now,	and	share
As	we	look	in - to	the	future	it's	as	far	as	we	can	see,	so	let's

57

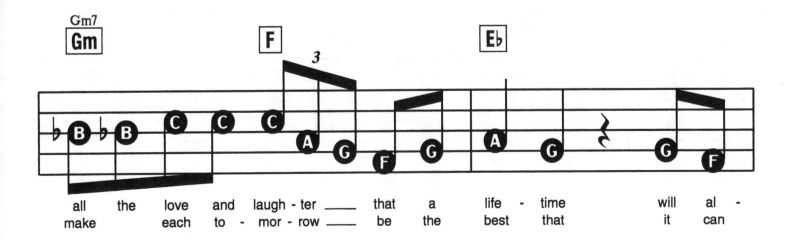

all the love and laugh - ter _____ that a life - time will al -
make each to - mor - row _____ be the best that it can

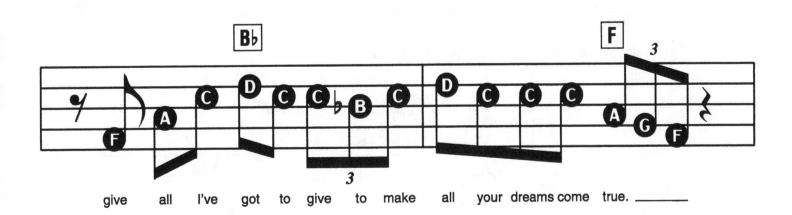

low. }
be. }
I cross my heart and prom - ise to

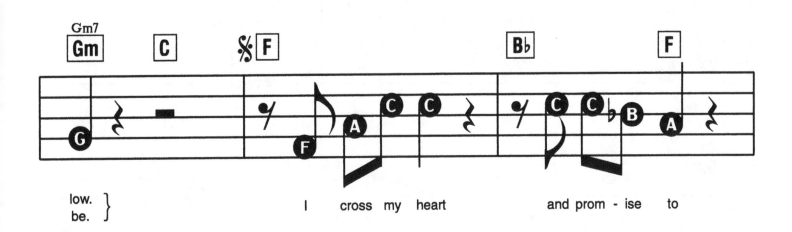

give all I've got to give to make all your dreams come true. _____

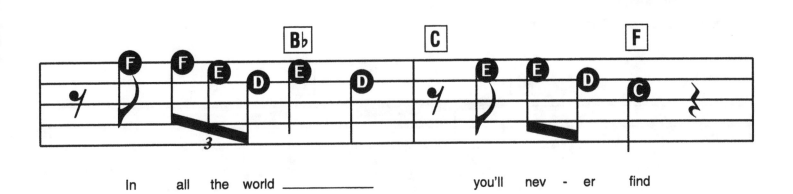

In all the world _____ you'll nev - er find

58

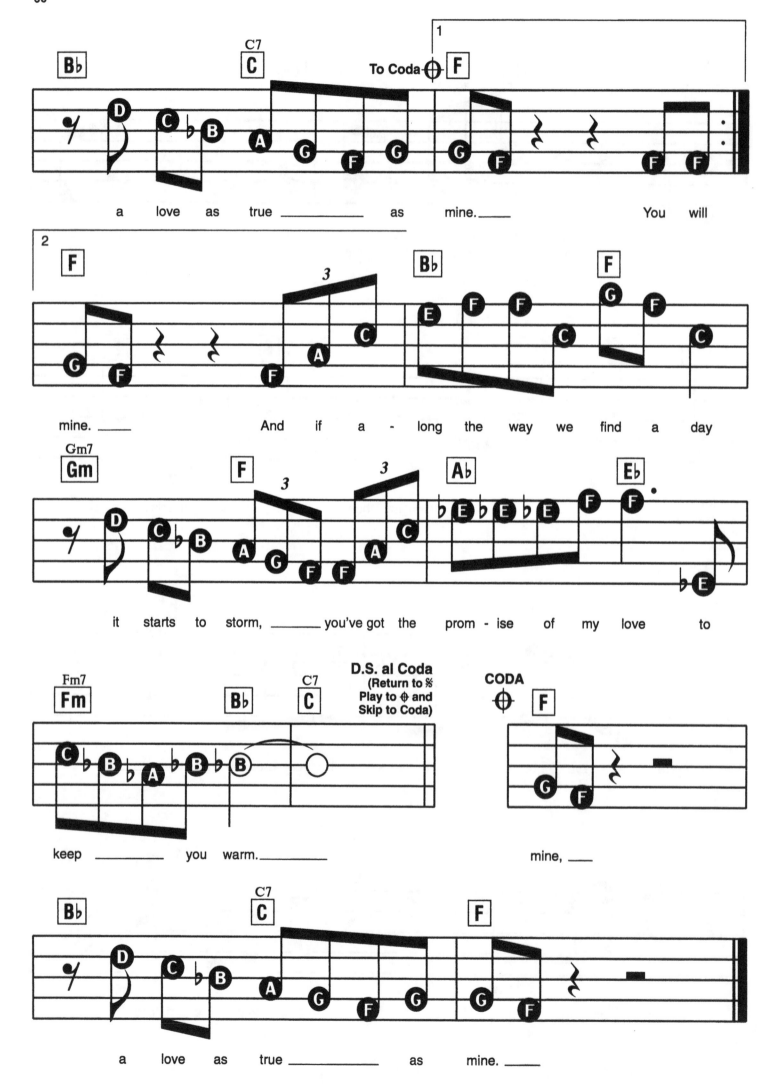

I'd Like to Have That One Back

Registration 1
Rhythm: 8 Beat or Ballad

Words and Music by Bill Shore,
Aaron Barker and Rick West

I heard some - bod - y speak her _____ name. _____ They
I can al - most see her stand - in' there, _____

said she was still look - in' fine.
tears she roll - in' down her face,

And I could feel that same old
as she packed a - way her

flame _____ I once felt when she was mine.
mem - 'ries _____ in that old worn out suit - case.

MCA music publishing

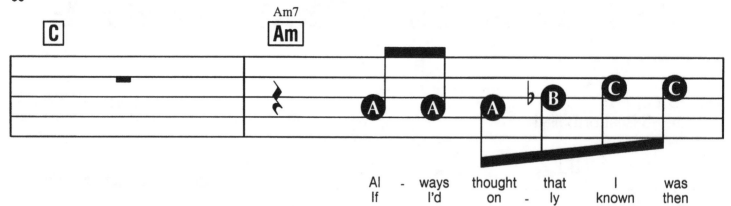

Al - ways thought that I was
If I'd on - ly known then

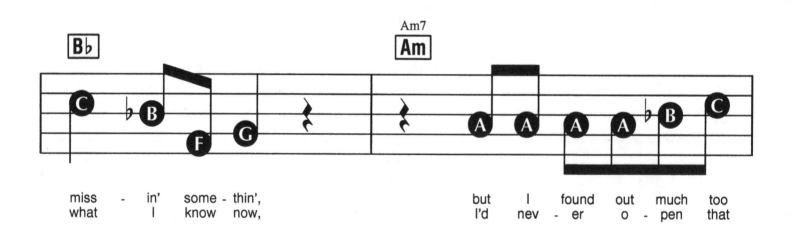

miss - in' some - thin',
what I know now,

but I found out much too
I'd nev - er o - pen that

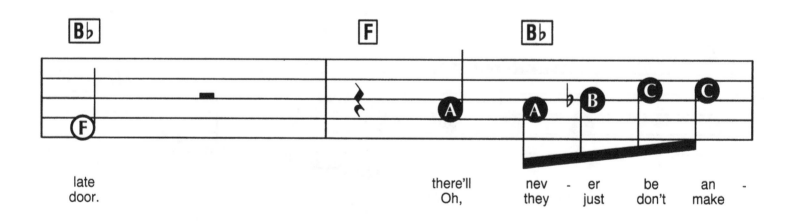

late
door.

there'll nev - er be an -
Oh, they just don't make

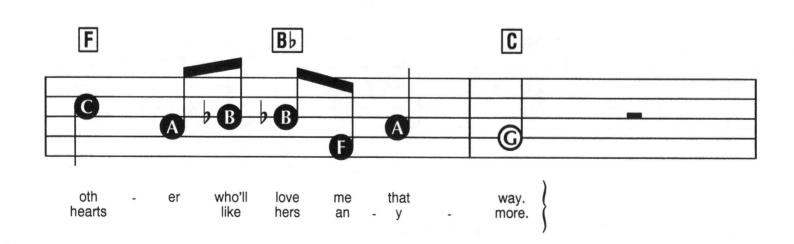

oth - er who'll love me that way.
hearts like hers an - y - more.

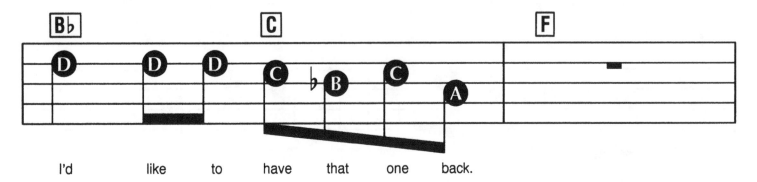

I'd like to have that one back.

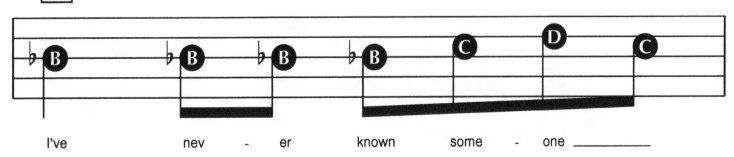

I've nev - er known some - one _____

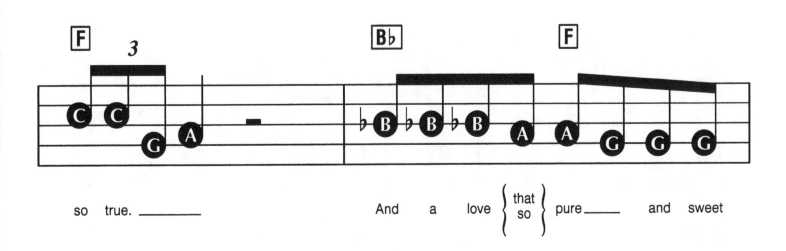

so true. _____   And a love { that / so } pure____ and sweet

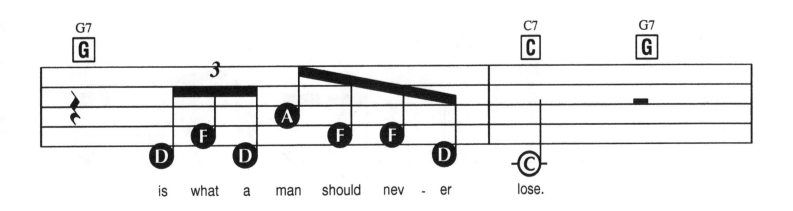

is what a man should nev - er lose.

62

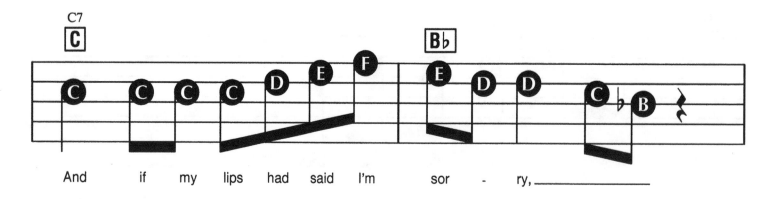

And if my lips had said I'm sor - ry, _____

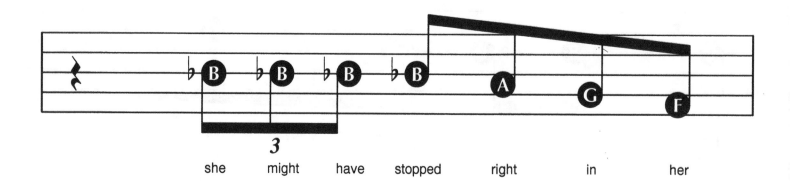

she might have stopped right in her

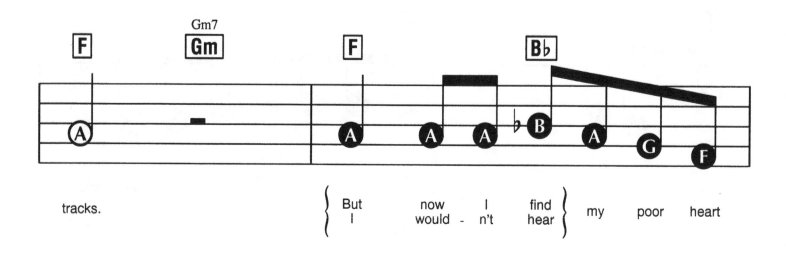

tracks.

{ But now I find }
{ I would - n't find hear } my poor heart

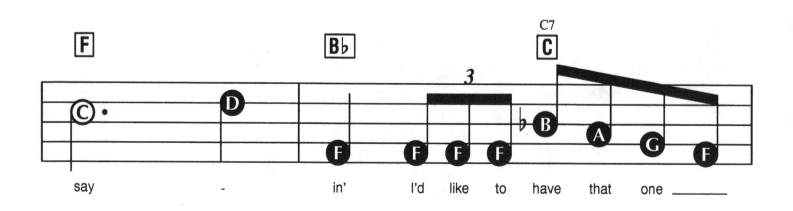

say - in' I'd like to have that one _____

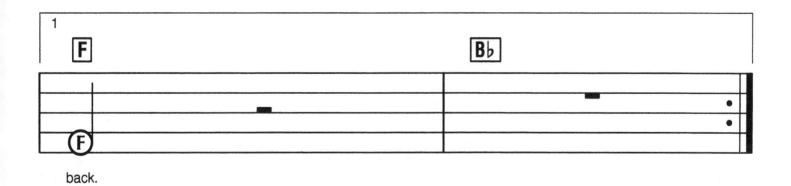

back.

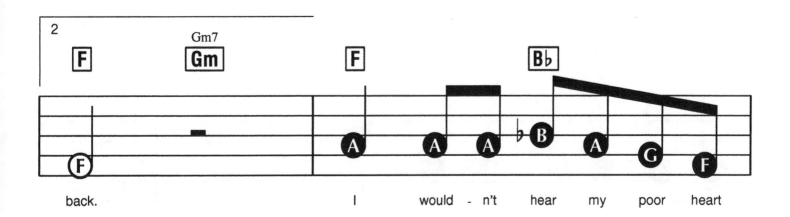

back.   I   would - n't   hear   my   poor   heart

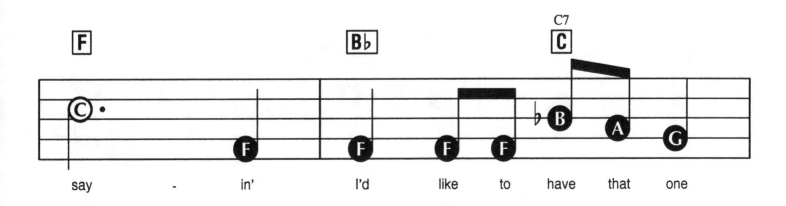

say   -   in'   I'd   like   to   have   that   one

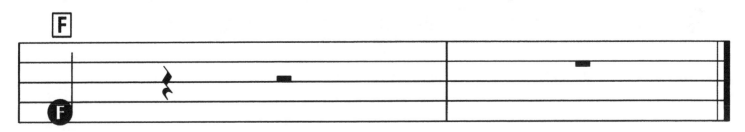

back.

I Know She Still Loves Me

Registration 3
Rhythm: Ballad

Words and Music by Aaron Barker
and Monty Holmes

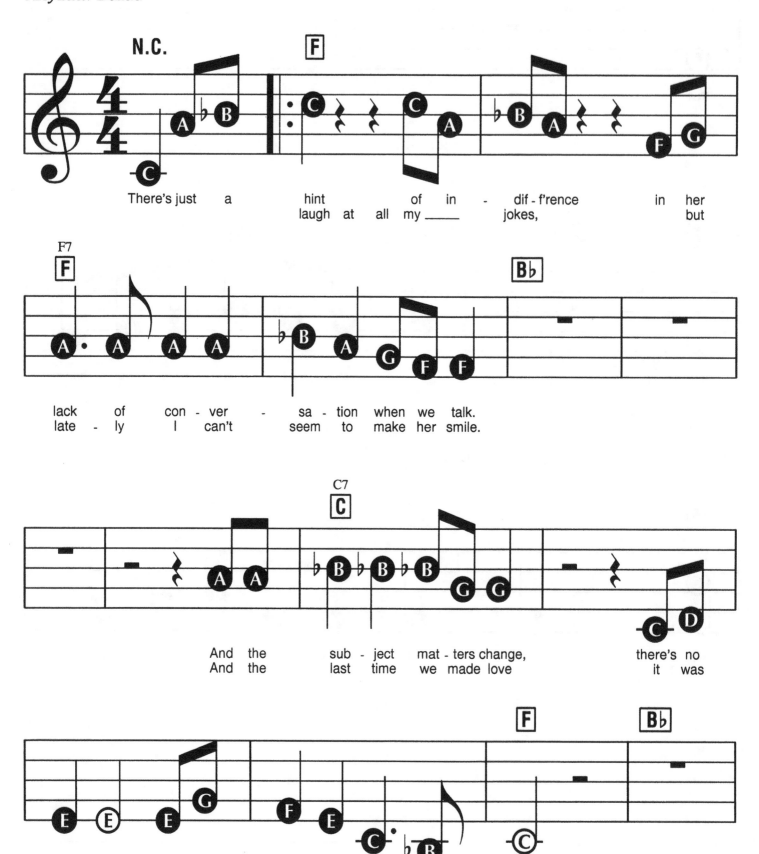

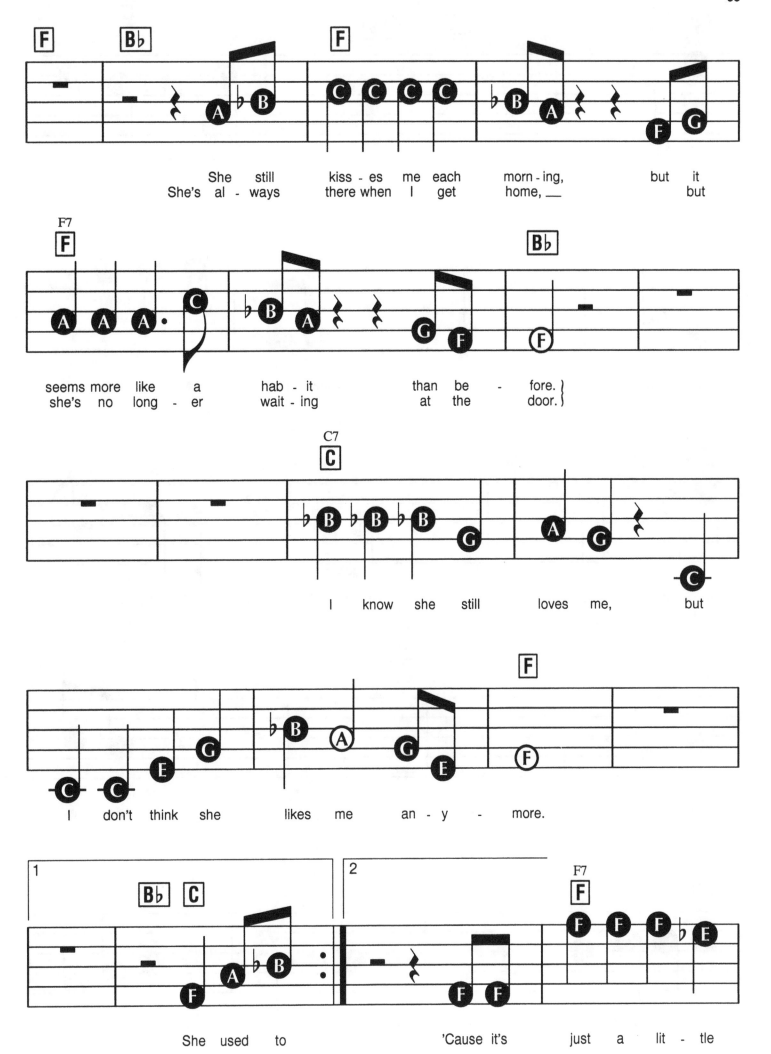

66

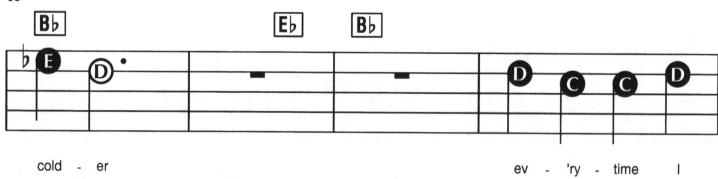

cold - er   ev - 'ry - time   I

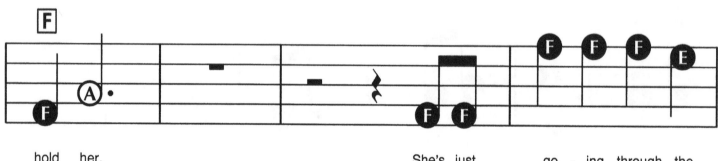

hold   her.   She's just   go - ing through the

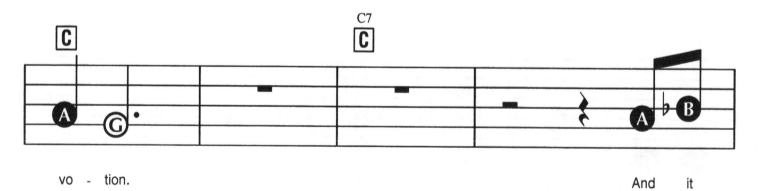

mo - tions _____   from what's   left   of   her   de -

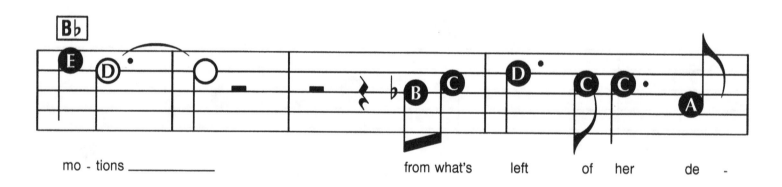

vo - tion.   And   it

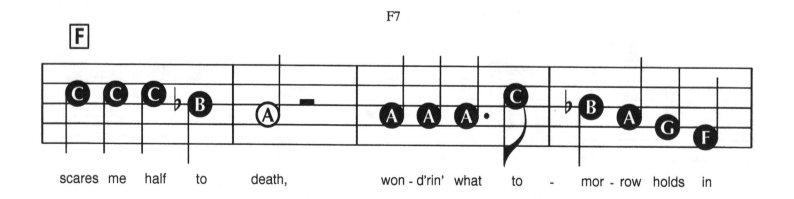

scares me   half   to   death,   won - d'rin' what   to - mor - row holds   in

67

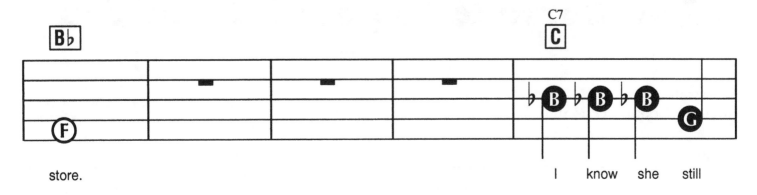

store.

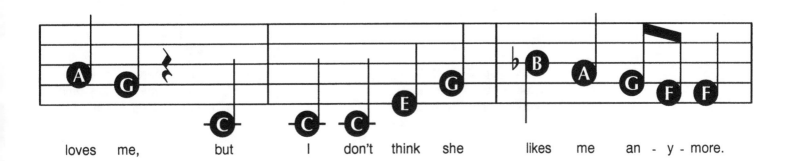

loves me, but I don't think she likes me an-y-more.

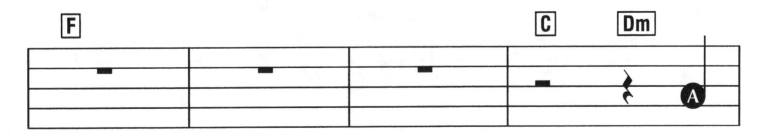

Right

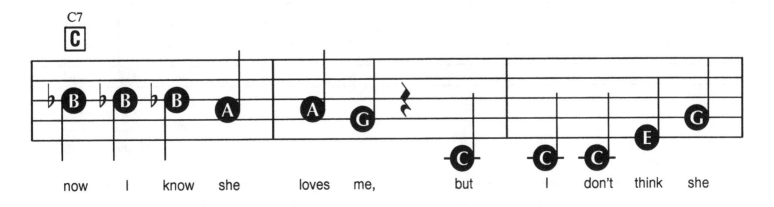

now I know she loves me, but I don't think she

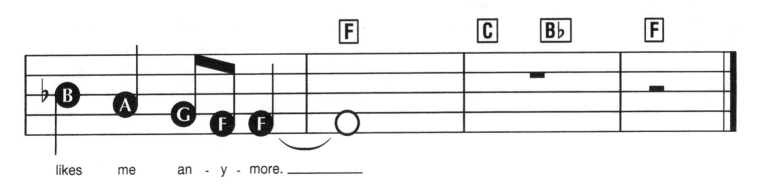

likes me an-y-more. _____

I've Come to Expect It from You

Registration 7
Rhythm: Country or March

Words and Music by Dean Dillon
and Buddy Cannon

MCA music publishing

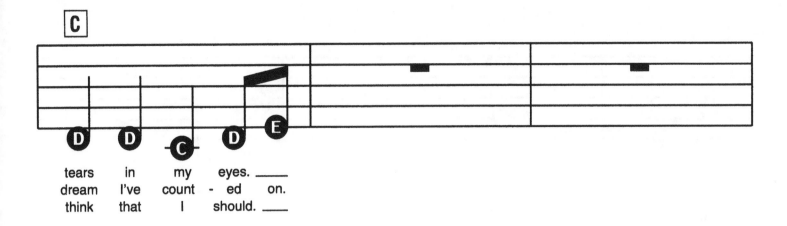

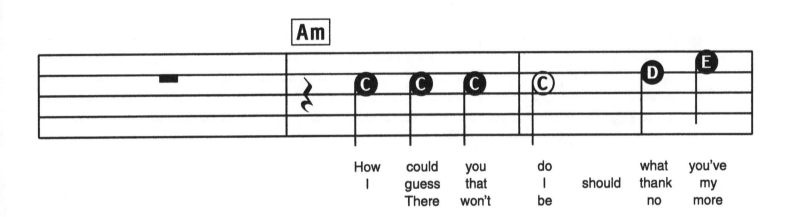

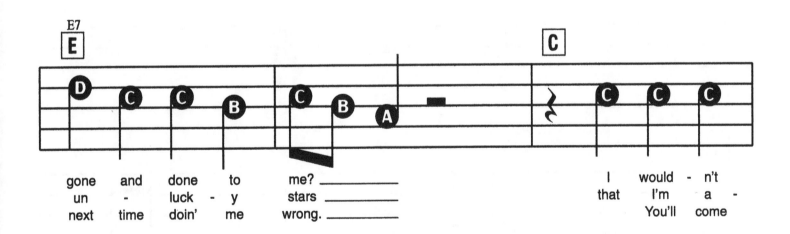

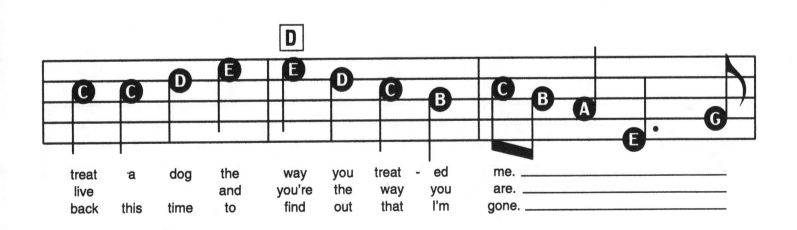

If I Know Me

Registration 7
Rhythm: Country or Pops

Words and Music by Dean Dillon
and Pam Belford

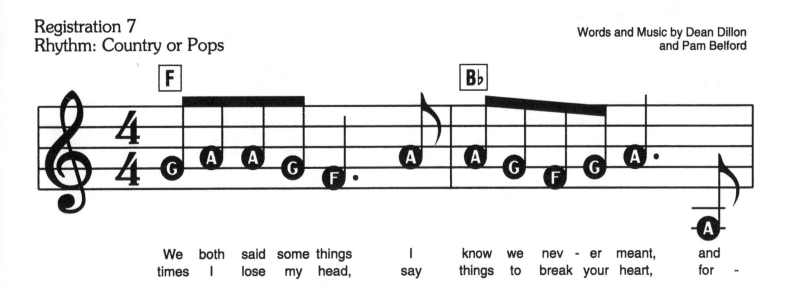

We both said some things I know we nev - er meant, and
times I lose my head, say things to break your heart, for -

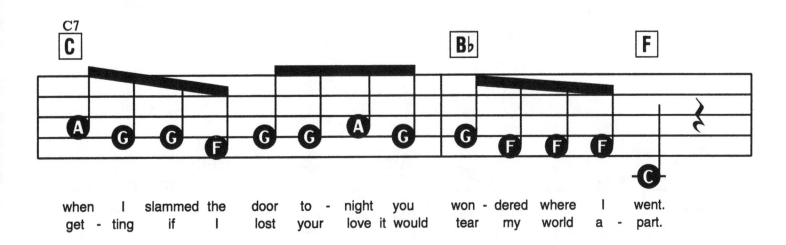

when I slammed the door to - night you won - dered where I went.
get - ting if I lost your love it would tear my world a - part.

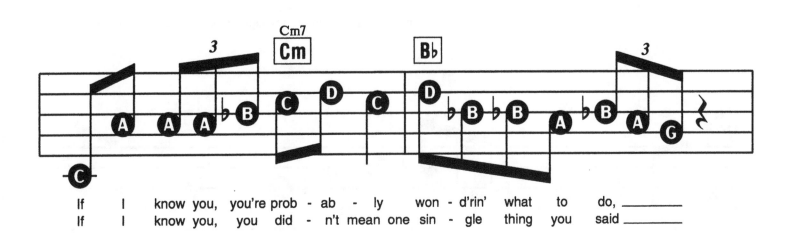

If I know you, you're prob - ab - ly won - d'rin' what to do, _____
If I know you, you did - n't mean one sin - gle thing you said _____

MCA music publishing

72

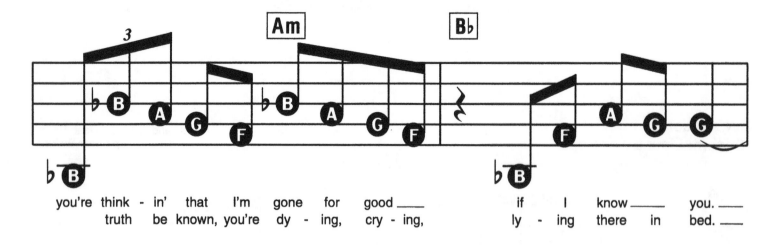

you're think - in' that I'm gone for good ____ if I know ____ you. ____
truth be known, you're dy - ing, cry - ing, ly - ing there in bed. ____

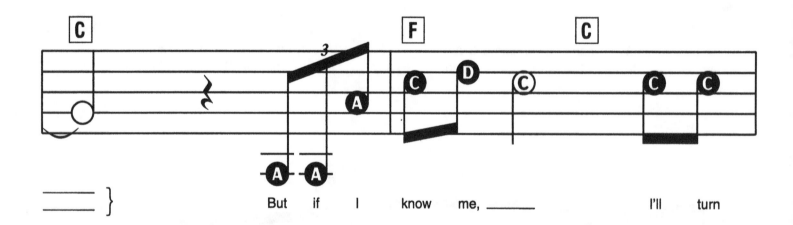

But if I know me, _____ I'll turn

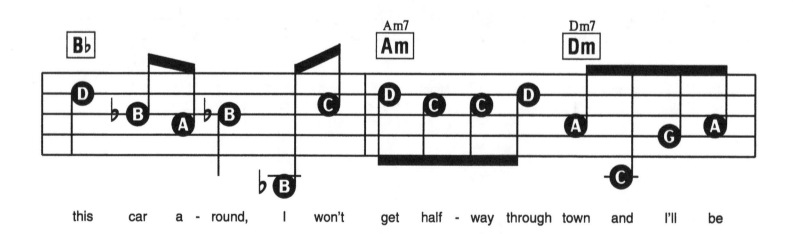

this car a - round, I won't get half - way through town and I'll be

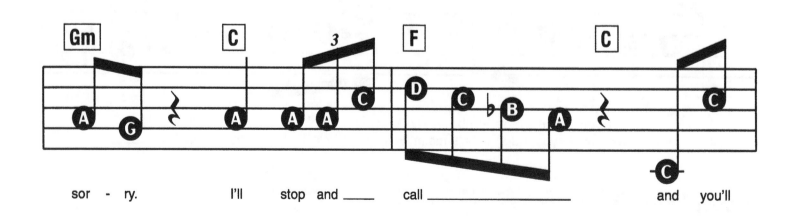

sor - ry. I'll stop and ____ call _____ and you'll

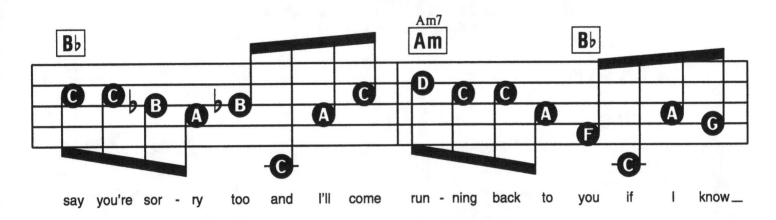

say you're sor - ry too and I'll come run - ning back to you if I know

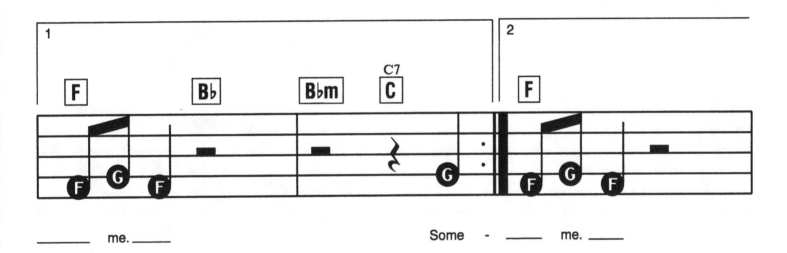

_____ me. _____ Some - ____ me. ____

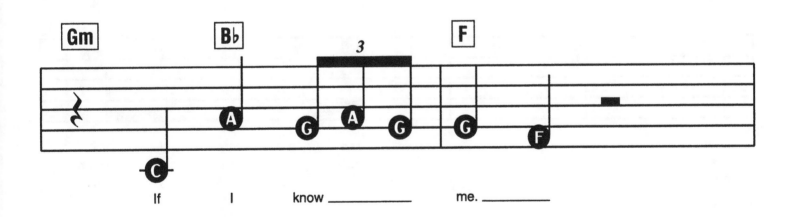

If I know _____ me. _____

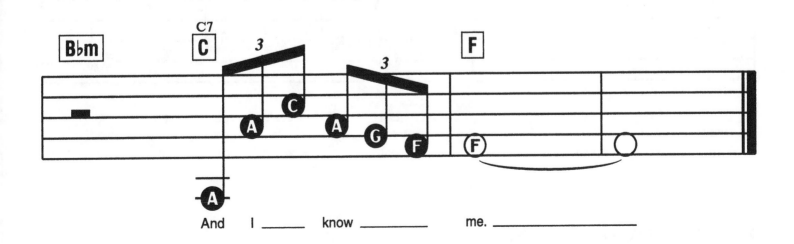

And I ____ know _____ me. _____

If You Ain't Lovin'
(You Ain't Livin')

Registration 3
Rhythm: Swing or Shuffle

Words and Music by
Tommy Collins

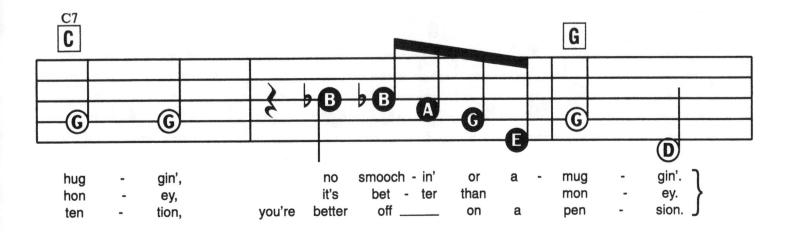

hug - gin', no smooch - in' or a - mug - gin'.
hon - ey, it's bet - ter than mon - ey.
ten - tion, you're better off ___ on a pen - sion.

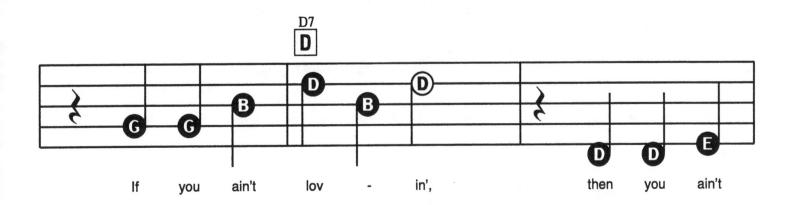

If you ain't lov - in', then you ain't

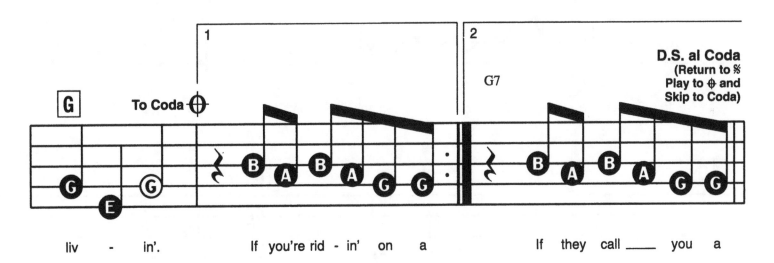

liv - in'. If you're rid - in' on a If they call ___ you a

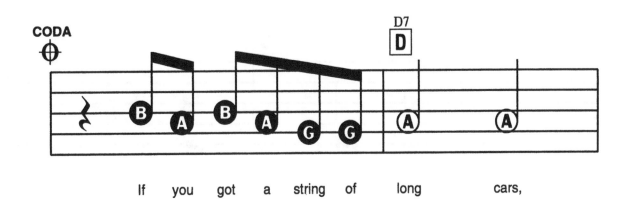

If you got a string of long cars,

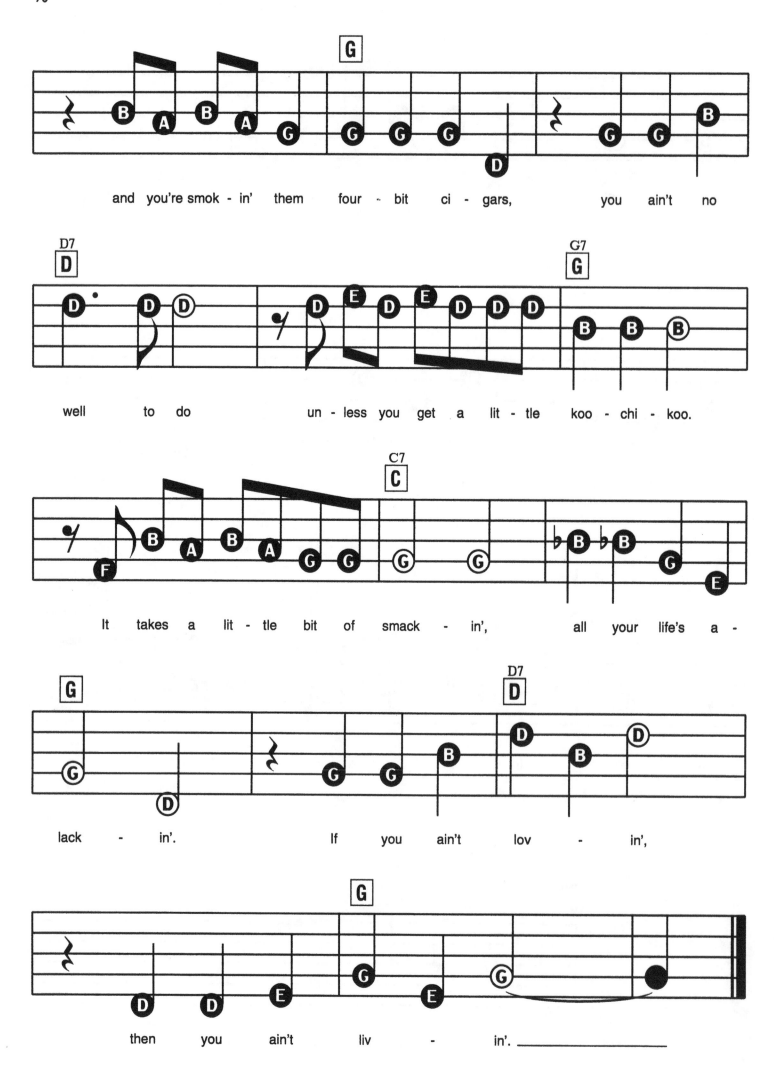

It Ain't Cool to Be Crazy About You

Registration 8
Rhythm: Pops or 8-Beat

Words and Music by Dean Dillon
and Royce Porter

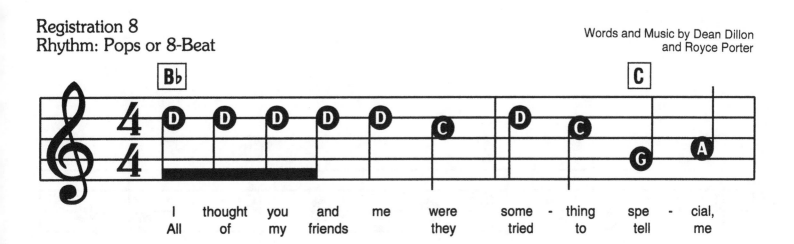

I thought you and me were some - thing spe - cial,
All of my friends they tried to tell me

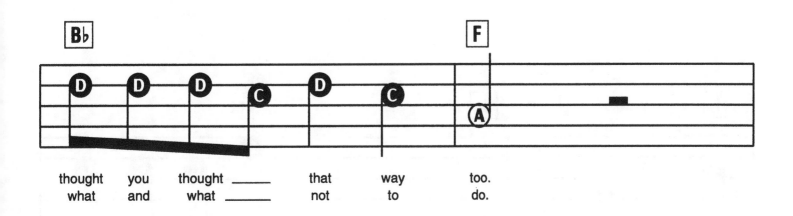

thought you thought _____ that way too.
what and what _____ not to do.

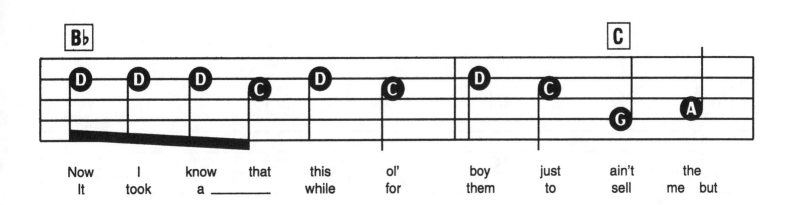

Now I know that this ol' boy just ain't the
It took a _____ while for them to sell me but

78

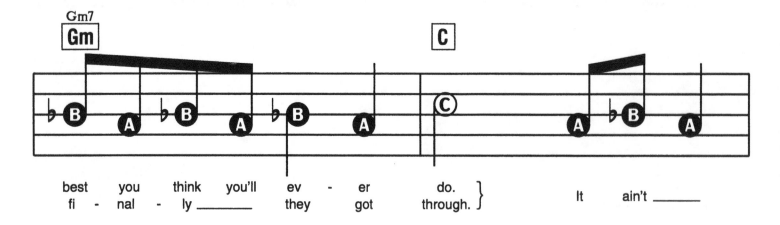

best   you   think   you'll   ev - er   do. }
fi - nal - ly _____ they   got   through. }   It   ain't _____

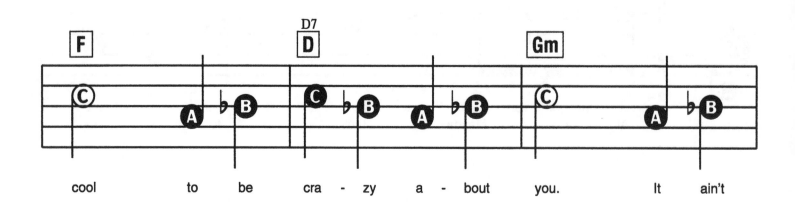

cool   to   be   cra - zy   a - bout   you.   It   ain't

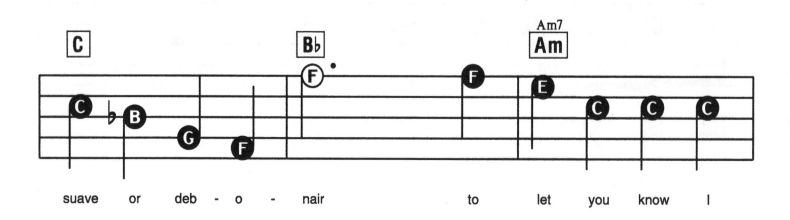

suave   or   deb - o - nair   to   let   you   know   I

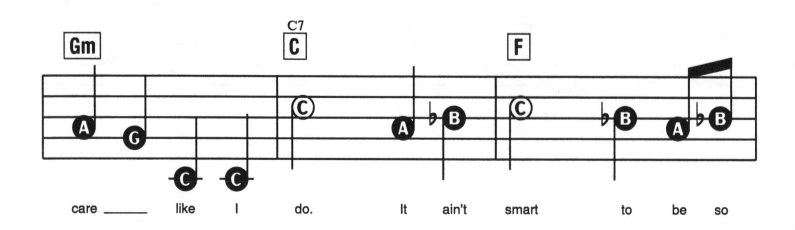

care _____ like   I   do.   It   ain't   smart   to   be   so

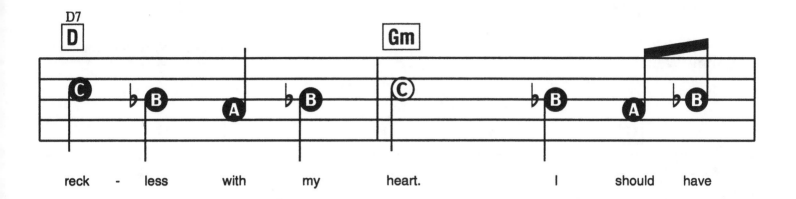

reck - less with my heart. I should have

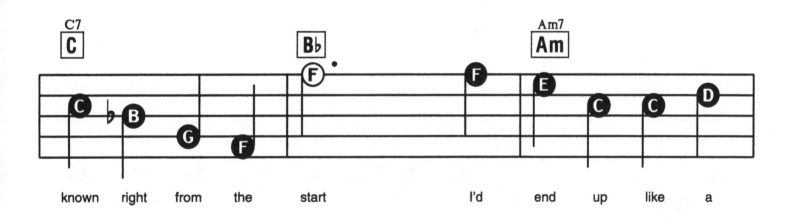

known right from the start I'd end up like a

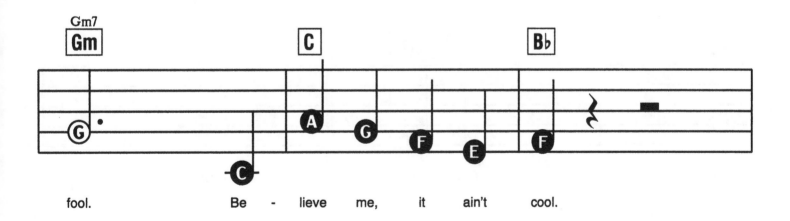

fool. Be - lieve me, it ain't cool.

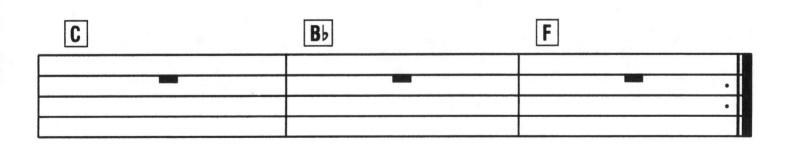

Let's Fall to Pieces Together

Registration 2
Rhythm: Waltz

Words and Music by Tommy Rocco,
Dickey Lee and Johnny Russell

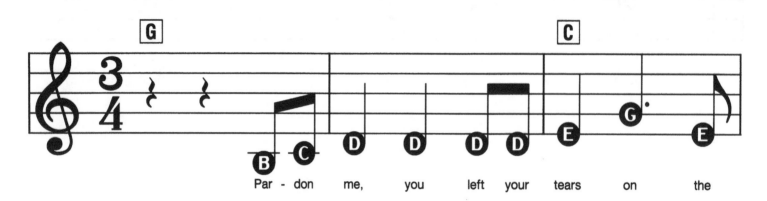

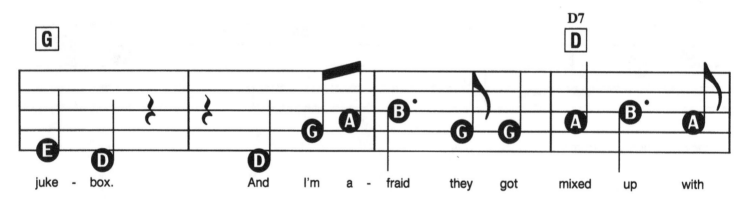

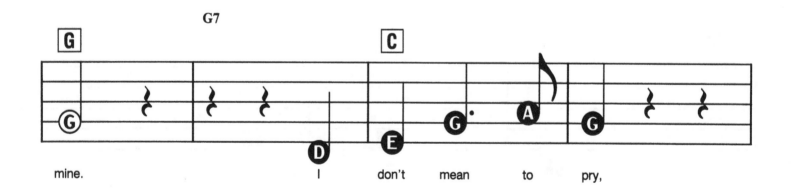

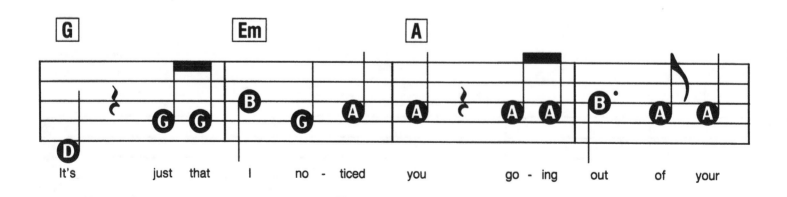

81

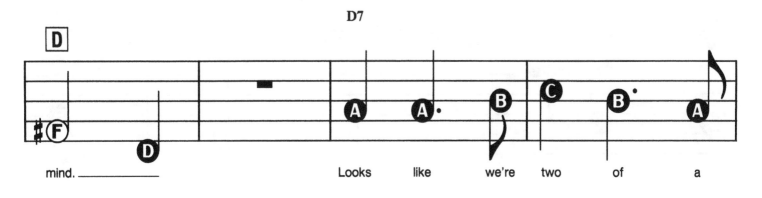

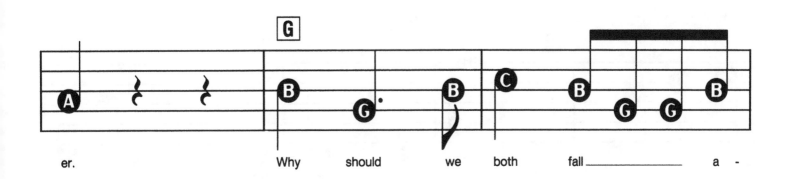

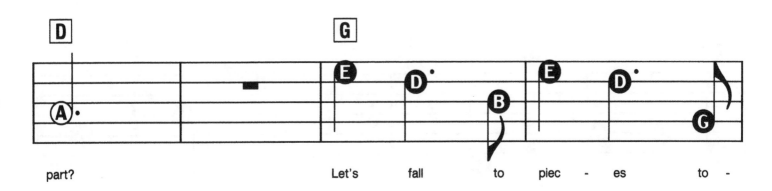

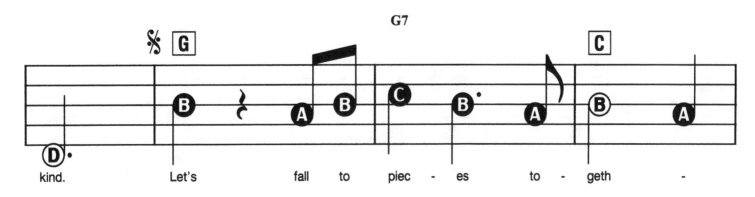

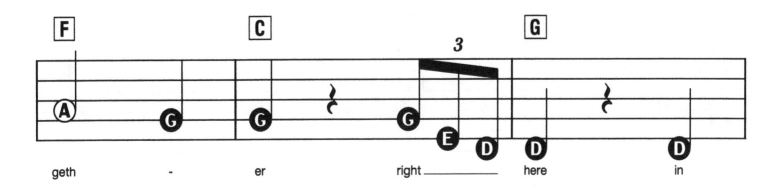

82

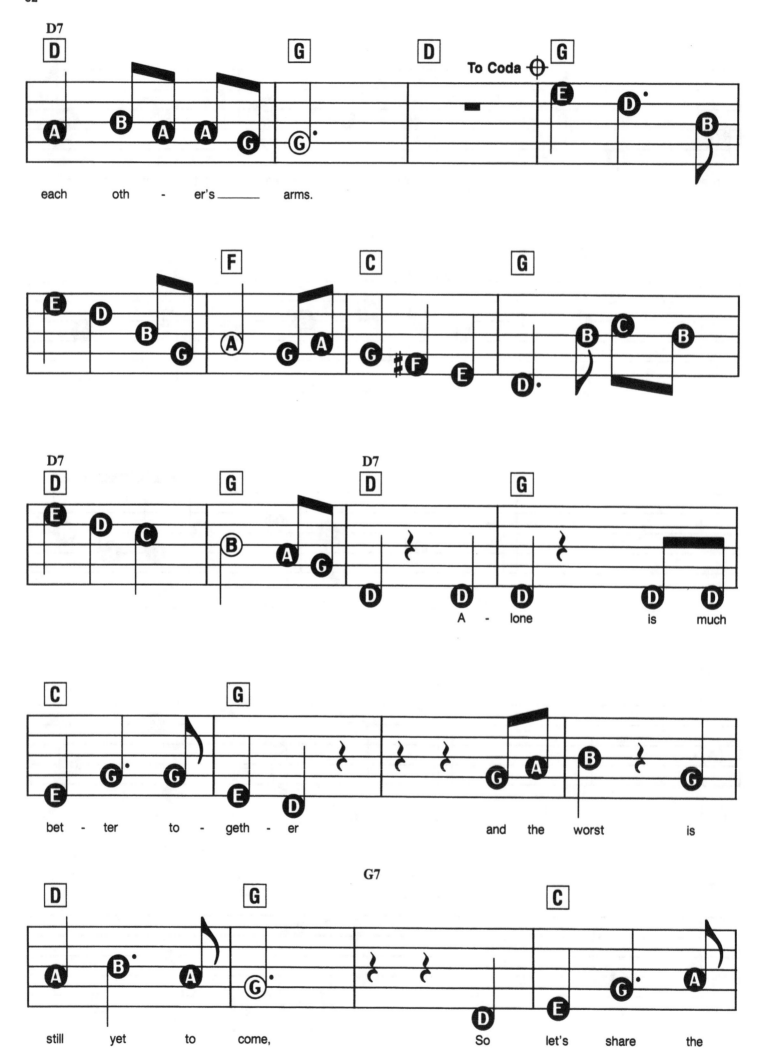

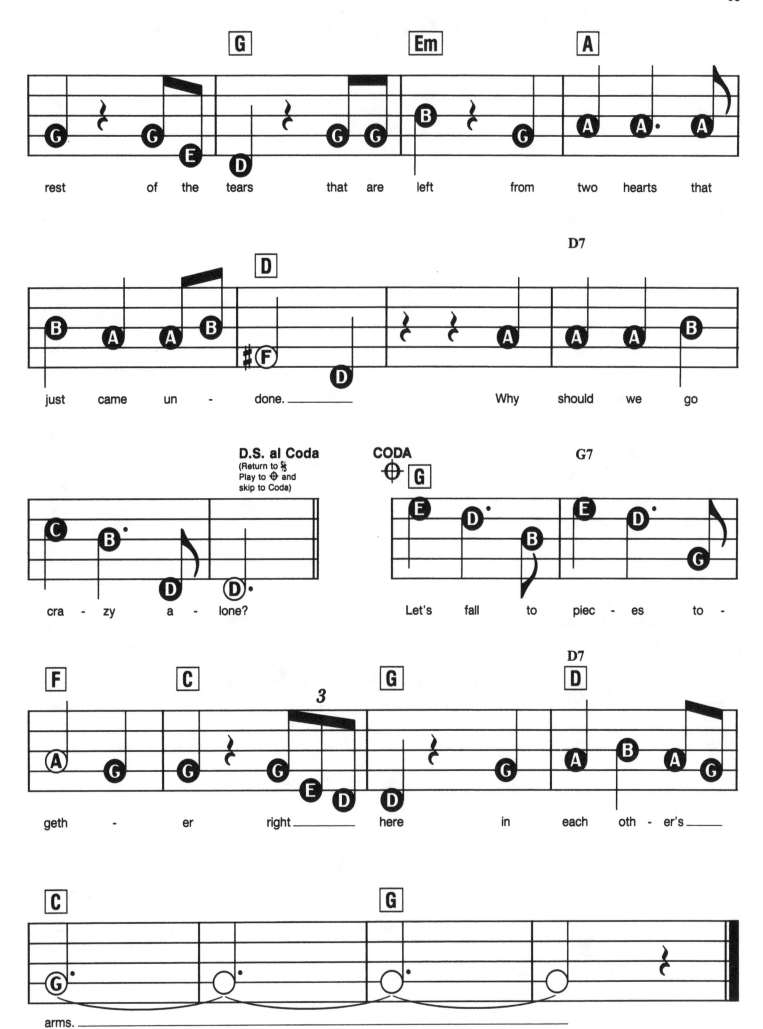

Love Without End, Amen

Registration 8
Rhythm: Country or Pops

Words and Music by
Aaron G. Barker

85

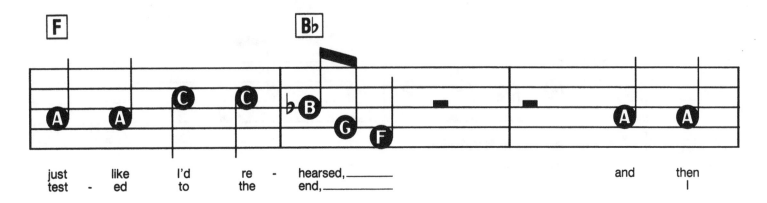

just like I'd re - hearsed,_____ and then
test - ed to the end,_____ I

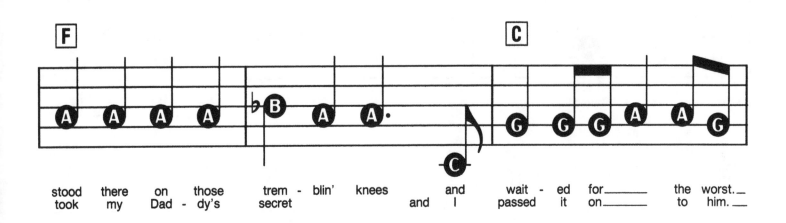

stood there on those trem - blin' knees and wait - ed for____ the worst.__
took my Dad - dy's secret and I passed it on____ to him. __

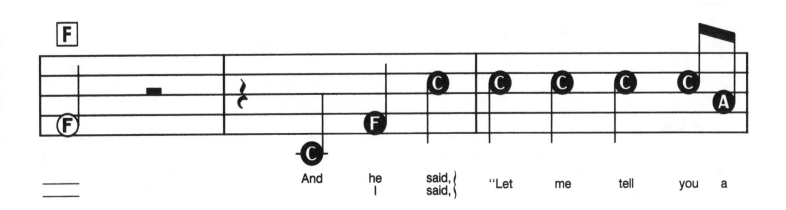

_____ And he said, { "Let me tell you a
_____ I said, {

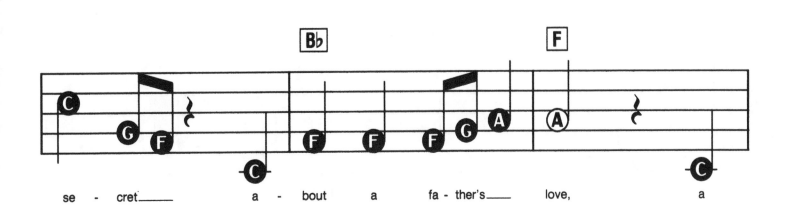

se - cret____ a - bout a fa - ther's____ love, a

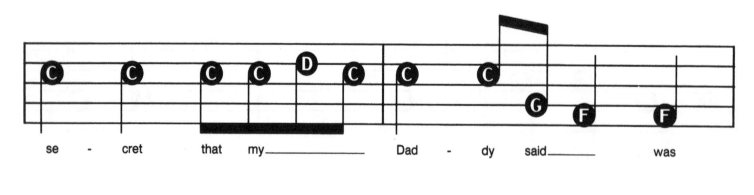

se - cret that my_____ Dad - dy said_____ was

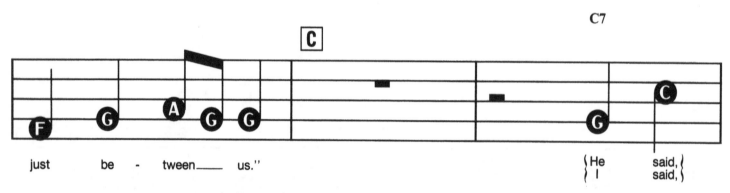

just be - tween____ us." {He said,} {I said,}

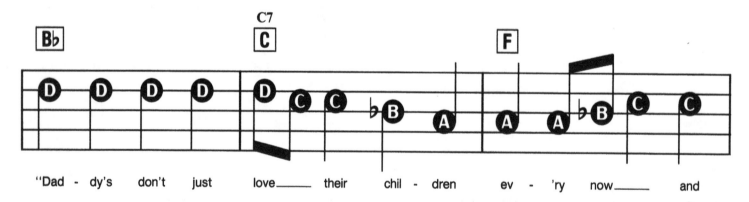

"Dad - dy's don't just love____ their chil - dren ev - 'ry now____ and

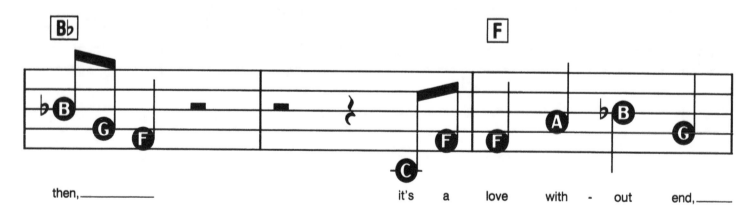

then,_____ it's a love with - out end,____

_____ A - men." It's a love with - out end,____

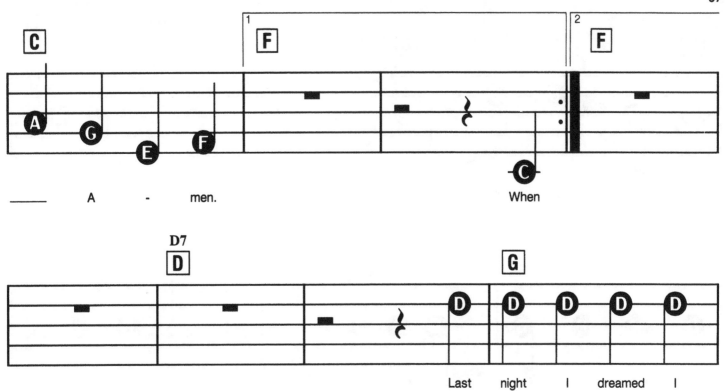

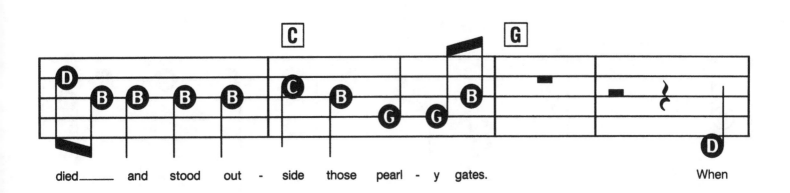

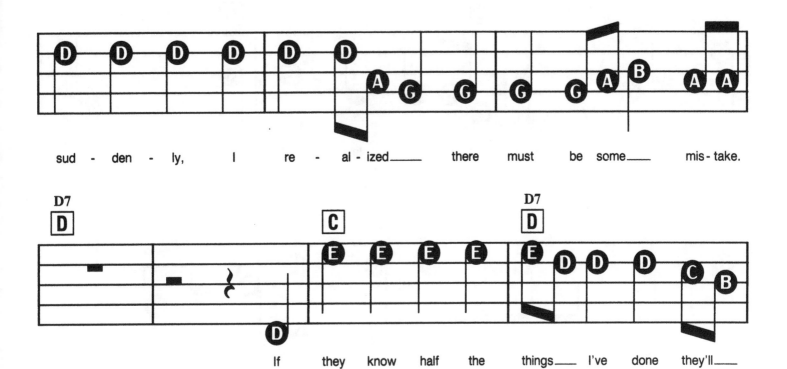

The Man in Love with You

Registration 2
Rhythm: 8 Beat or Pop

Words and Music by Stephen Dorff
and Gary Harju

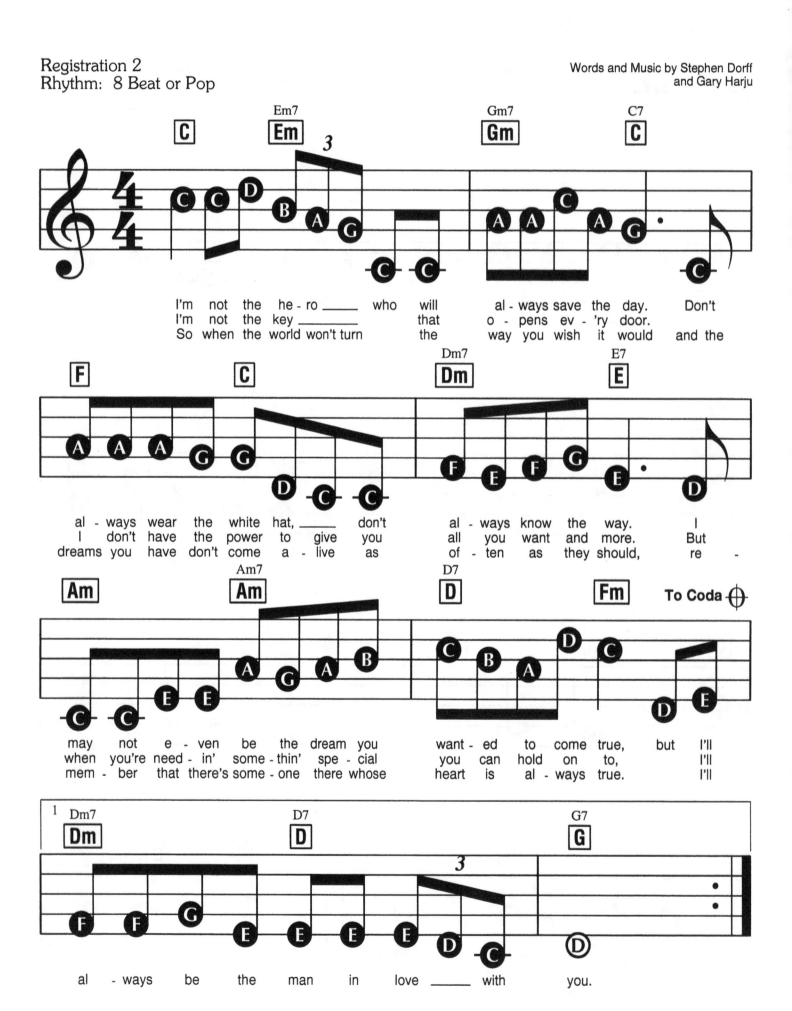

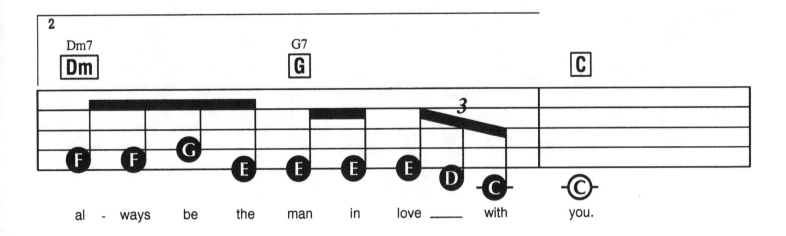

al - ways be the man in love ____ with you.

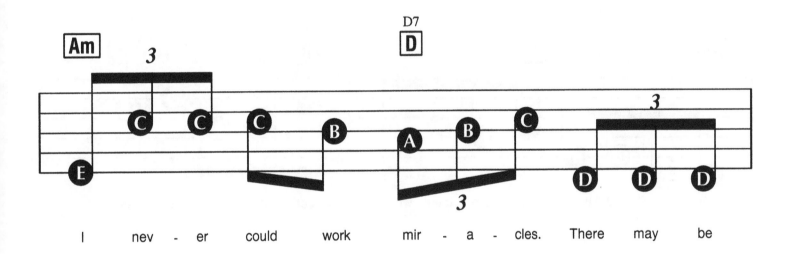

I nev - er could work mir - a - cles. There may be

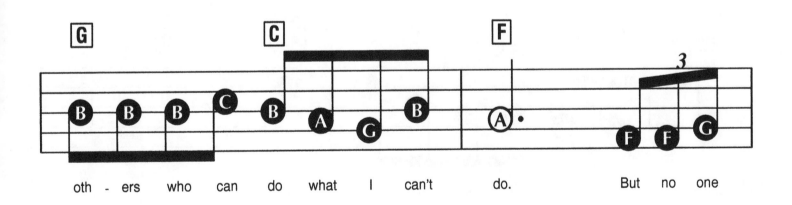

oth - ers who can do what I can't do. But no one

D.C. al Coda (Return to beginning
Play to ⊕ and
Skip to Coda)

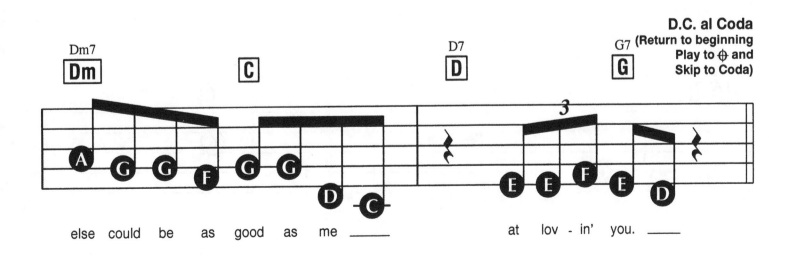

else could be as good as me ____ at lov - in' you. ____

CODA

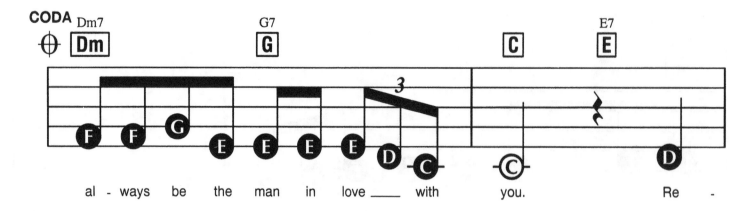

al - ways be the man in love _____ with you. Re -

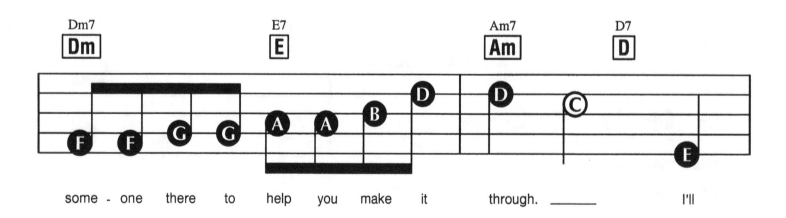

mem - ber that there's some - one there whose heart is al - ways true,

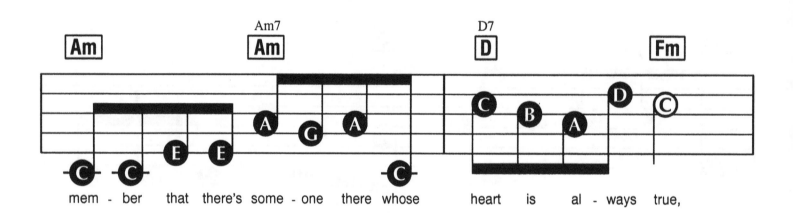

some - one there to help you make it through. _____ I'll

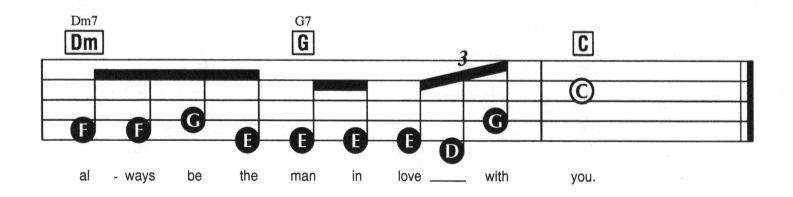

al - ways be the man in love _____ with you.

Nobody in His Right Mind Would've Left Her

Registration 3
Rhythm: Pops or 8 Beat

Words and Music by
Dean Dillon

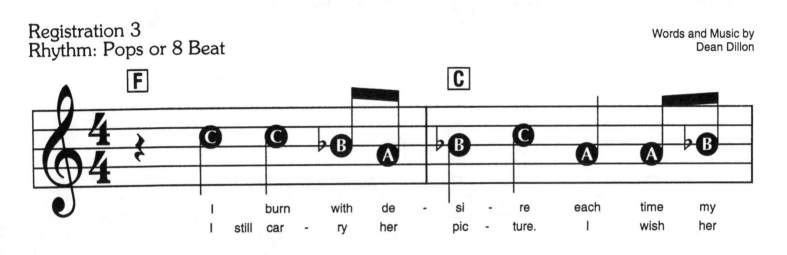

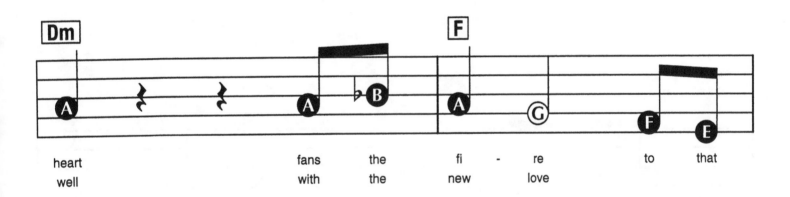

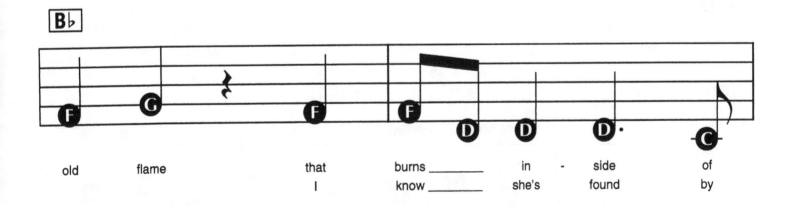

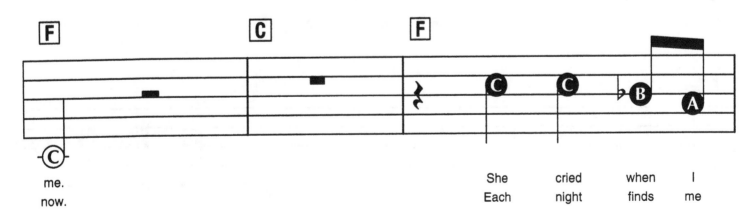

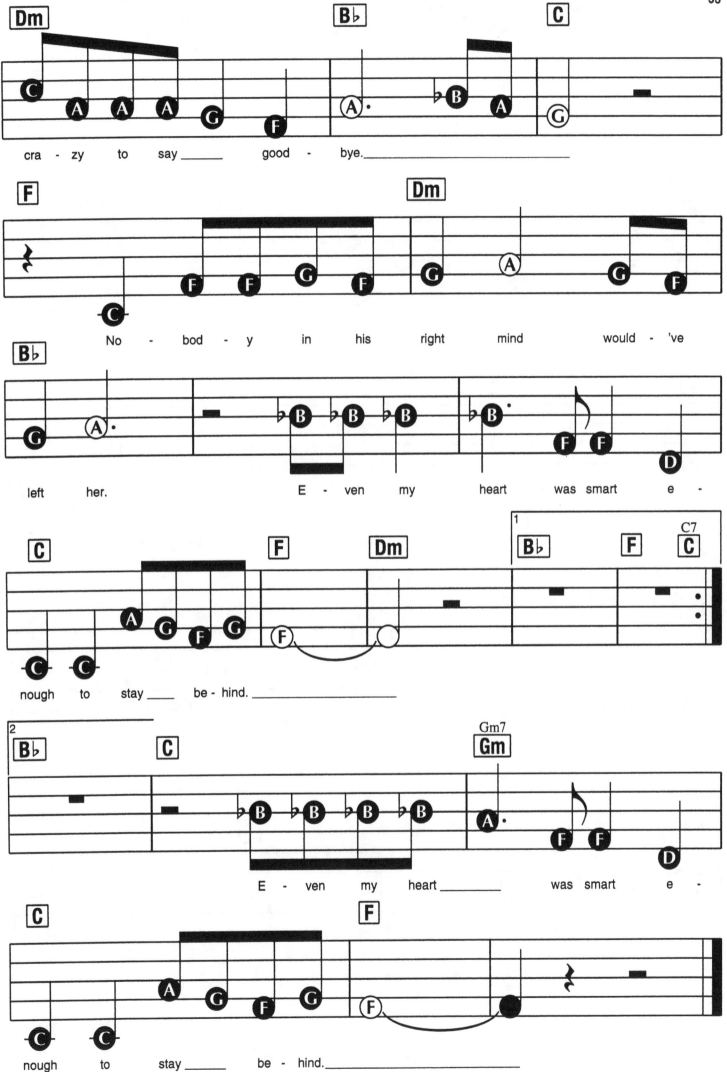

Ocean Front Property

Registration 3
Rhythm: Country or Swing

Words and Music by Hank Cochran,
Royce Porter and Dean Dillon

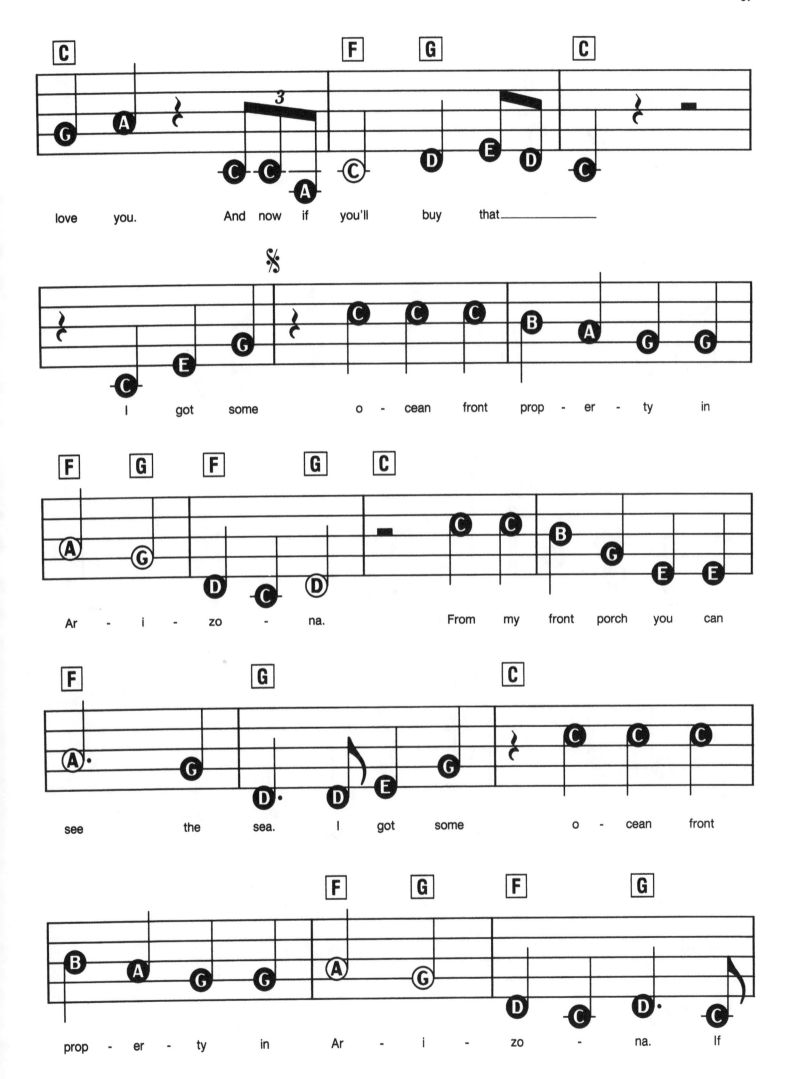

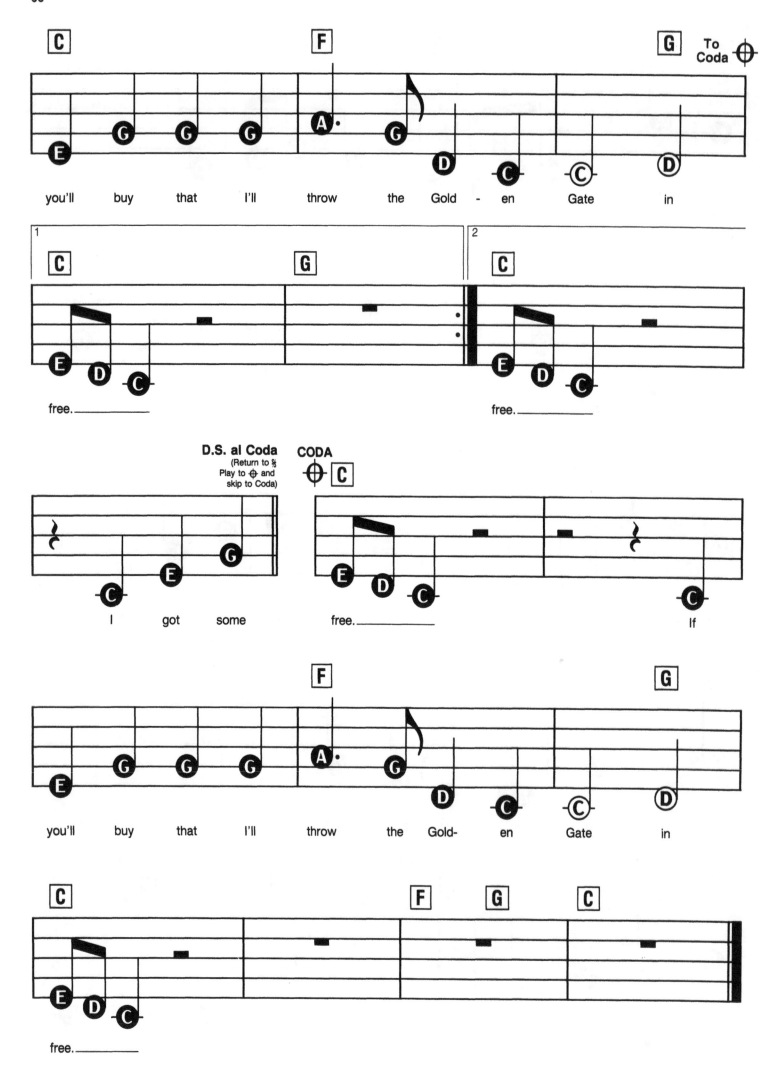

Right or Wrong

Registration 3
Rhythm: Swing or Big Band

Lyric by Haven Gillespie
Music by Arthur Sizemore and Paul Biese

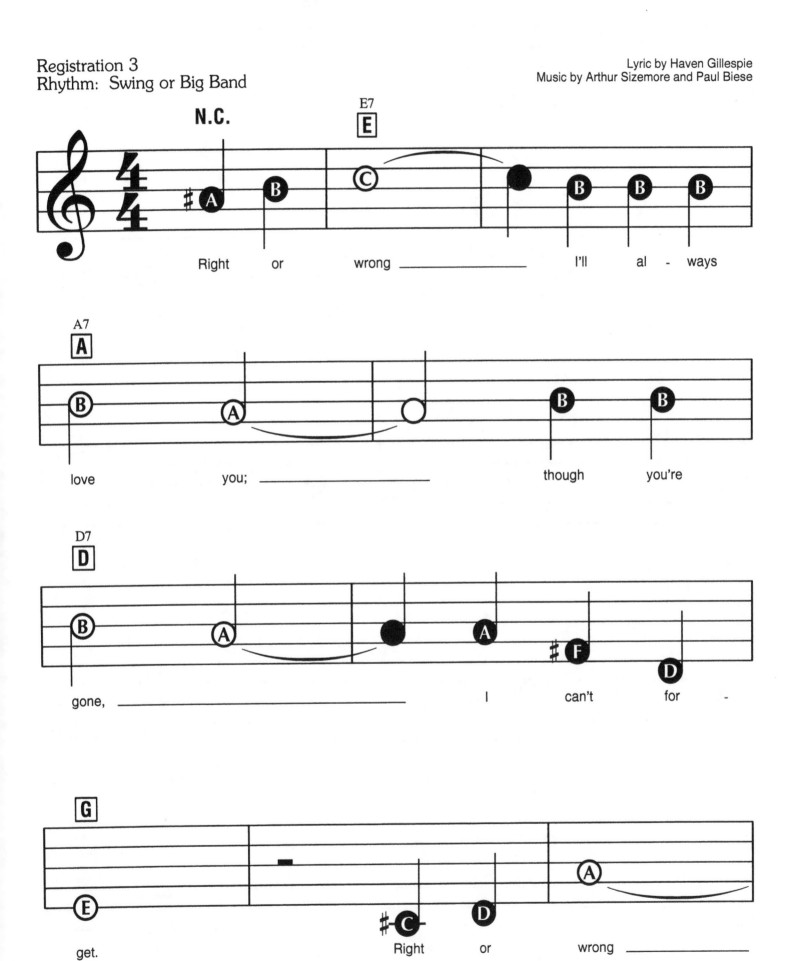

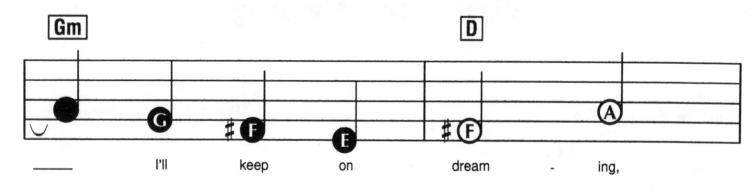

I'll keep on dream - ing,

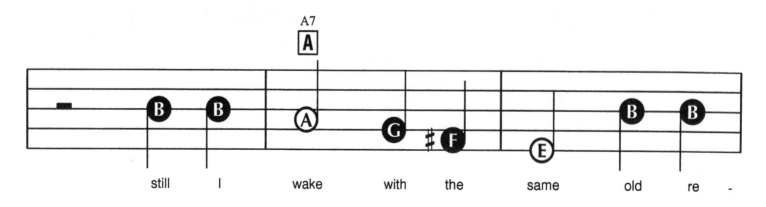

still I wake with the same old re -

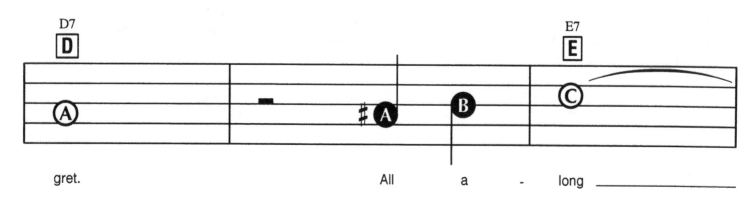

gret. All a - long ____

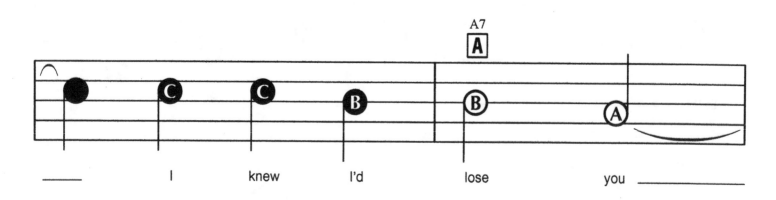

____ I knew I'd lose you ____

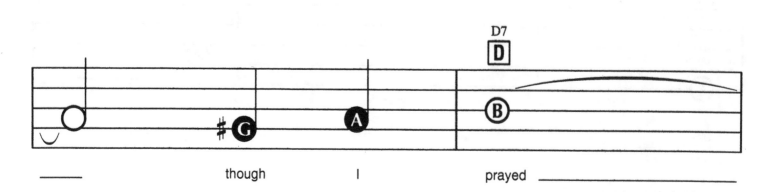

____ though I prayed ____

101

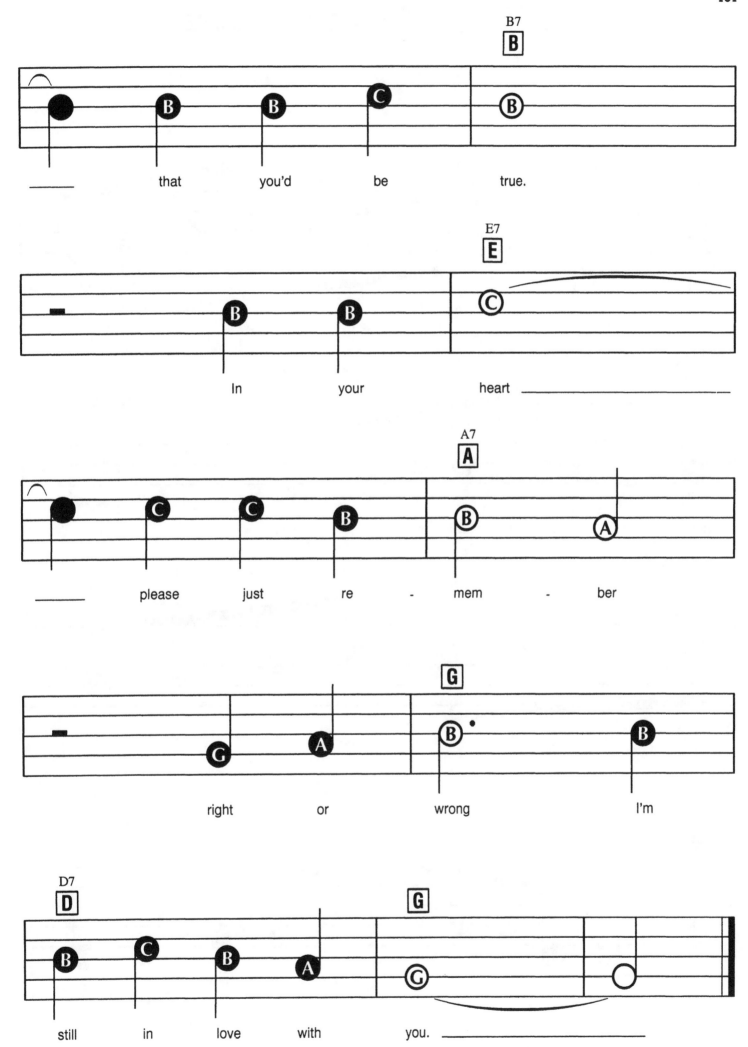

So Much Like My Dad

Registration 1
Rhythm: Ballad or 8 Beat

Words and Music by Chips Moman
and Bobby Emmons

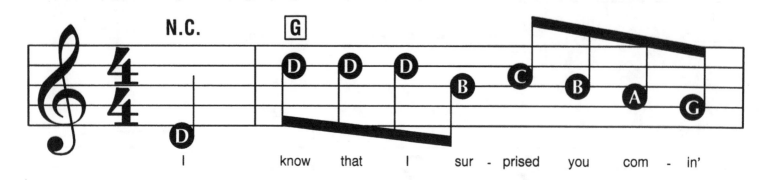

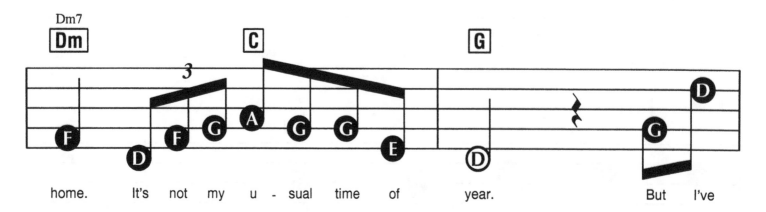

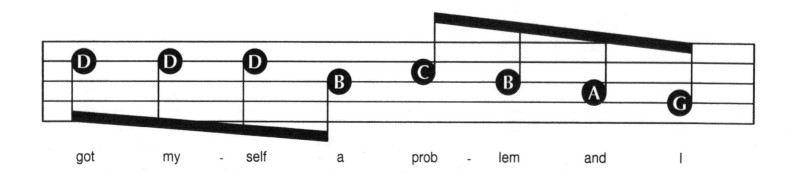

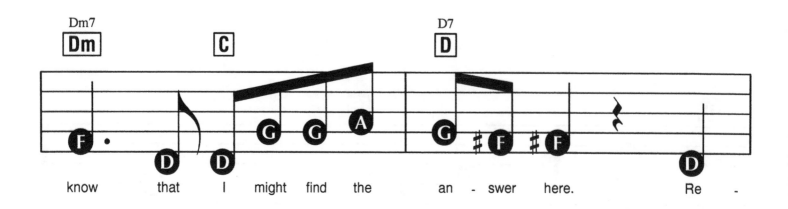

103

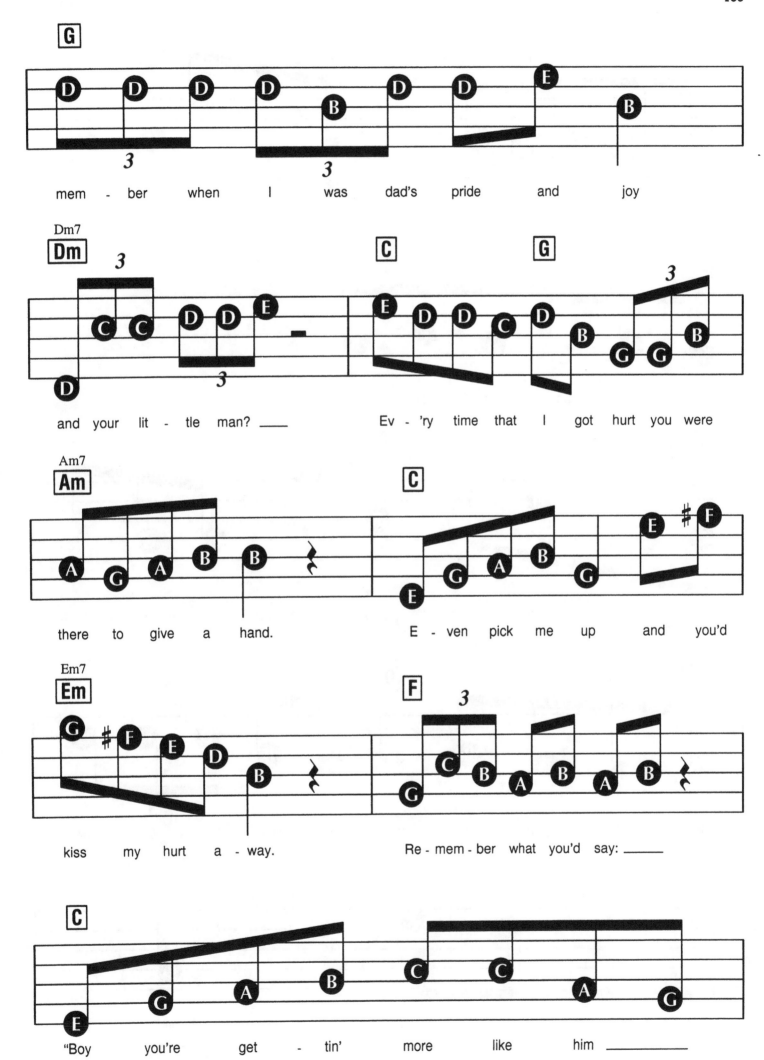

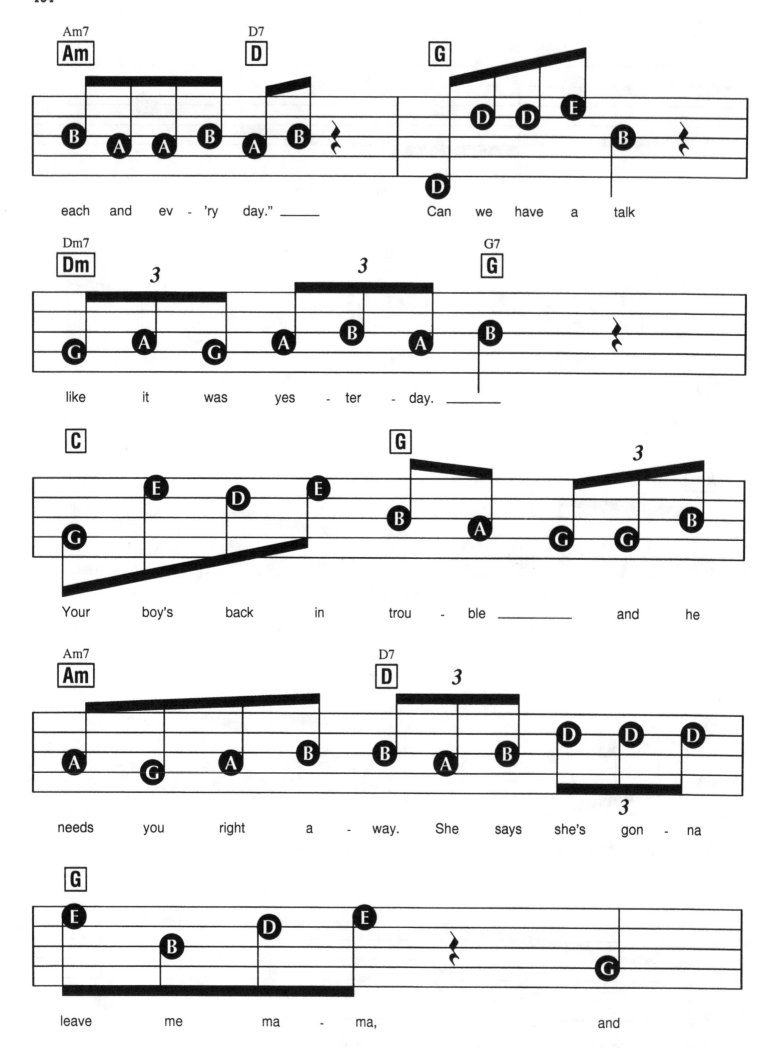

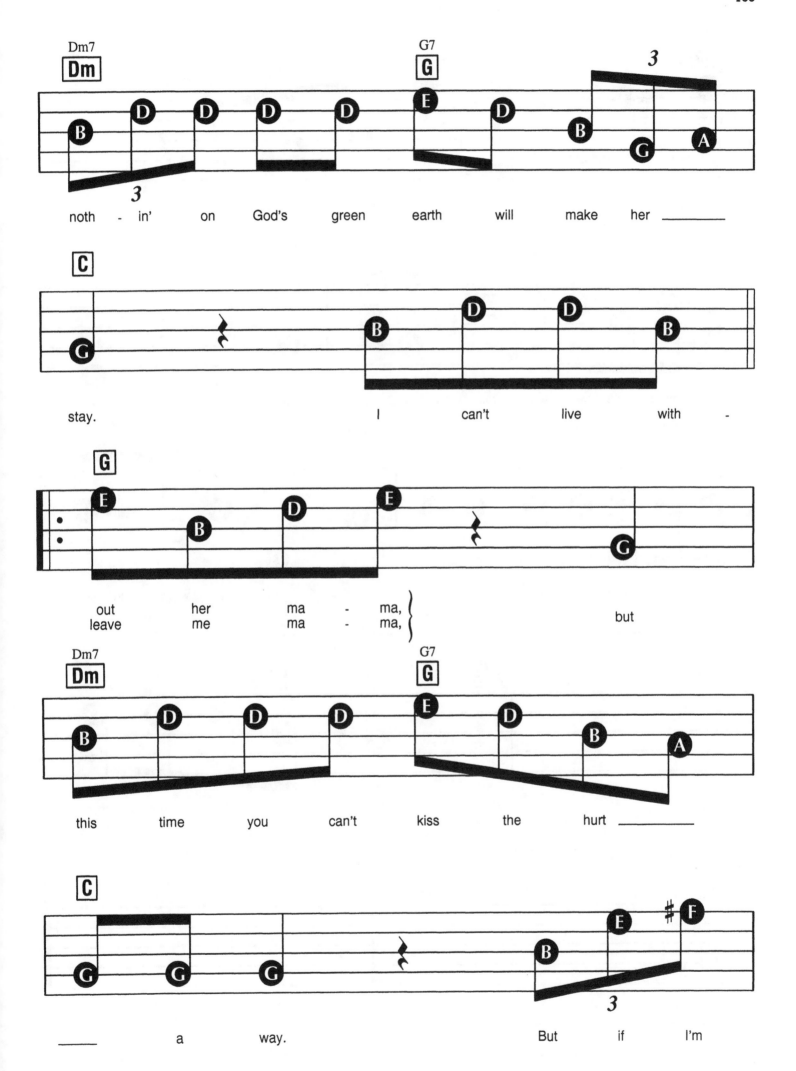

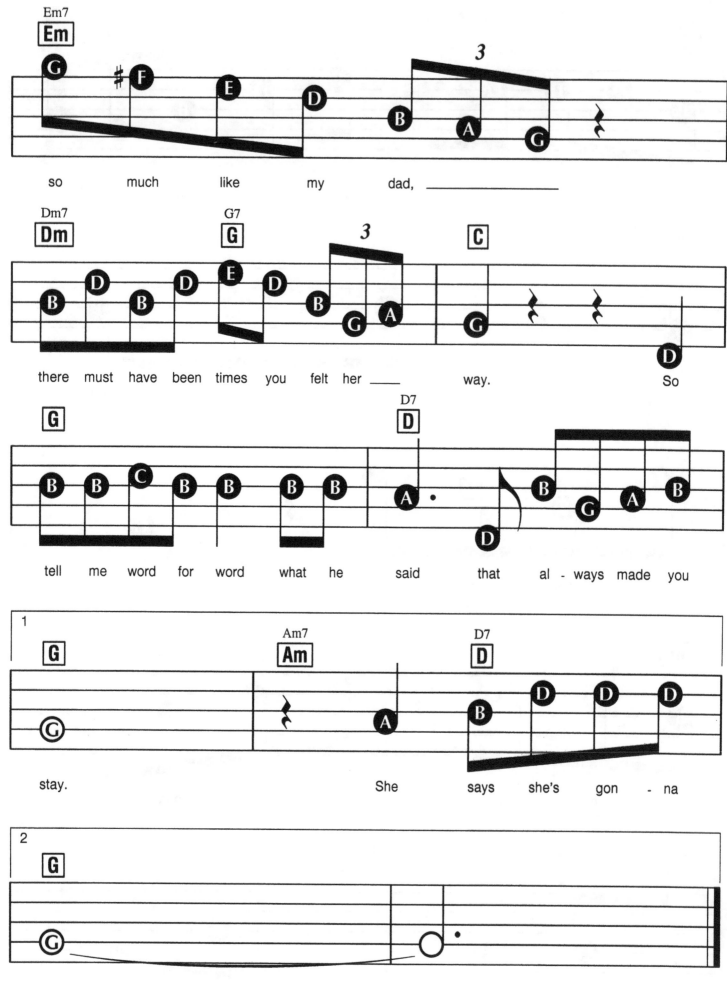

so   much   like   my   dad, _____

there must have been times you felt her ___   way.   So

tell   me   word   for   word   what   he   said   that   al - ways made   you

stay.   She   says   she's   gon - na

stay. _____

What's Going on in Your World

Registration 10
Rhythm: Shuffle or Bounce

Words and Music by David Chamberlain,
Royce Porter and Red Steagall

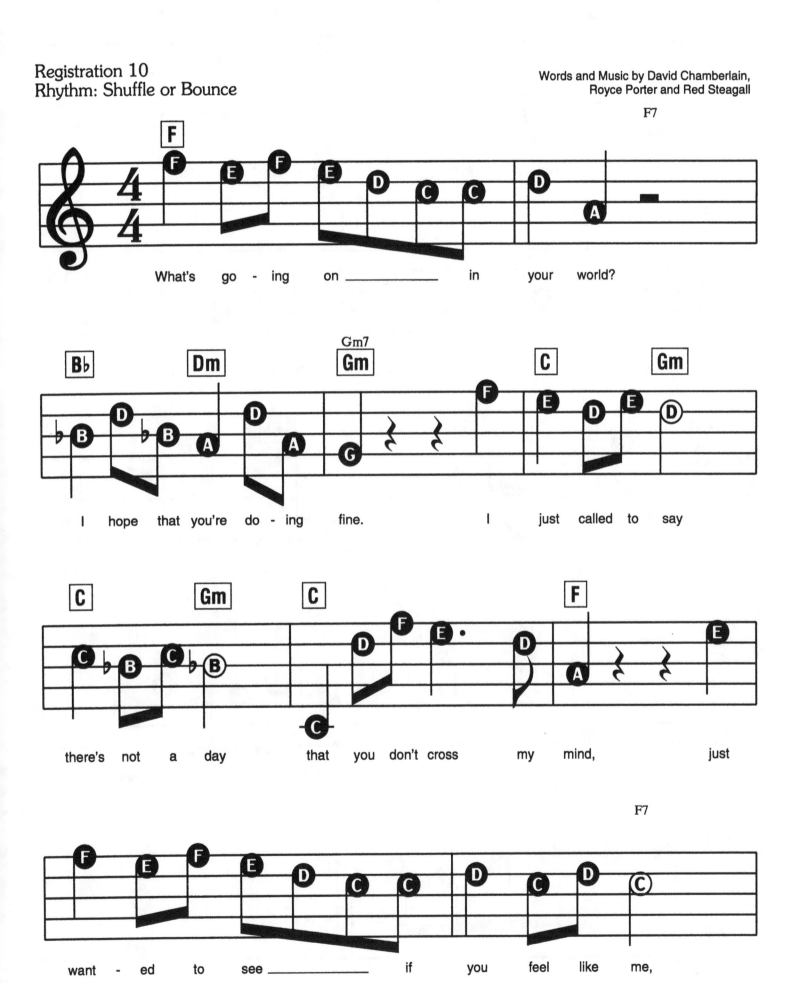

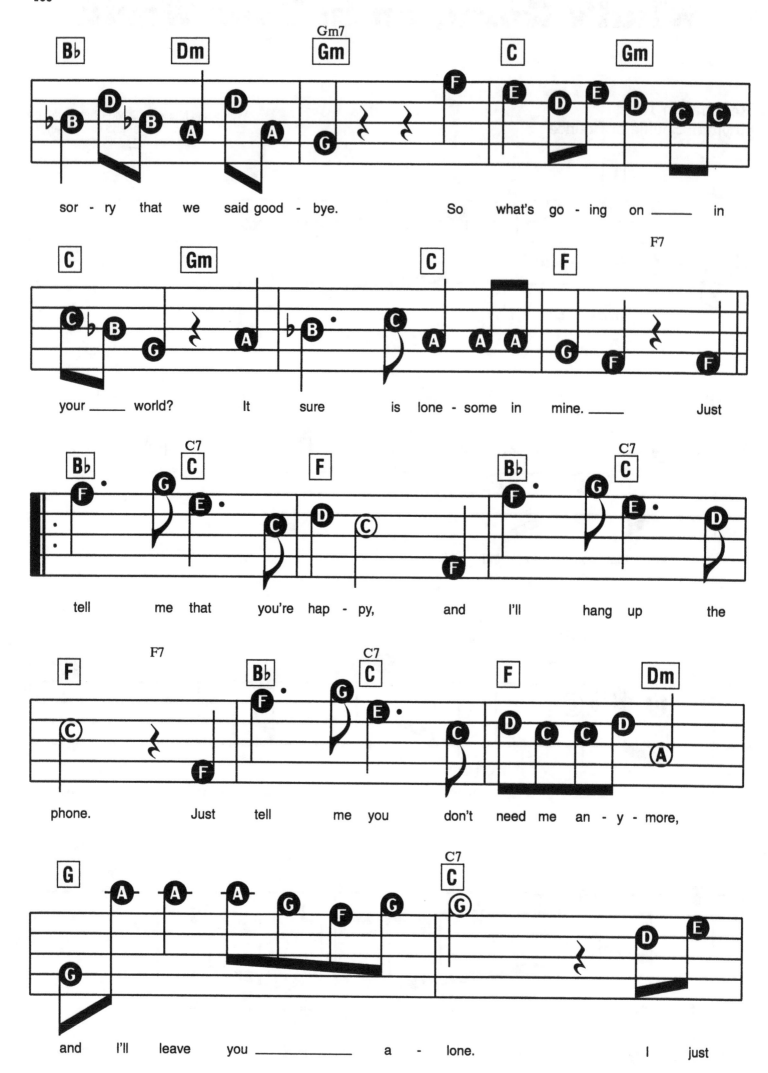

sor - ry that we said good - bye. So what's go - ing on _____ in

your _____ world? It sure is lone - some in mine. _____ Just

tell me that you're hap - py, and I'll hang up the

phone. Just tell me you don't need me an - y - more,

and I'll leave you _____ a - lone. I just

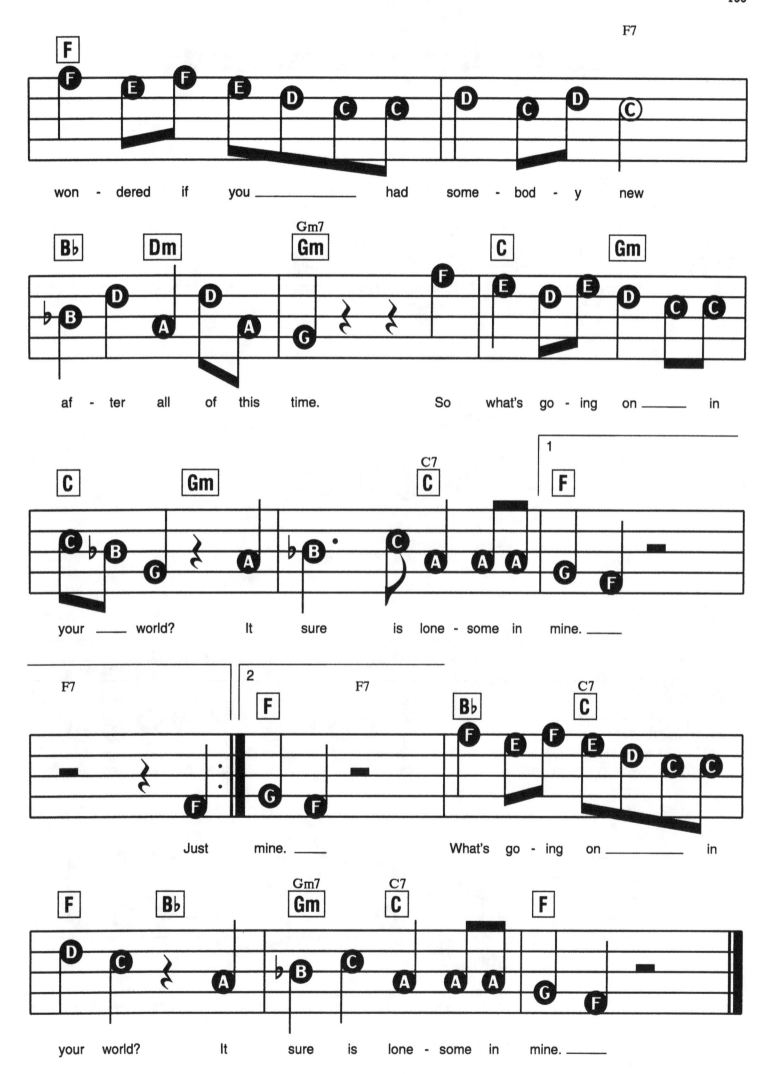

You Can't Make a Heart Love Somebody

Registration 7
Rhythm: Ballad

Words and Music by Steve Clark
and Johnny MacRae

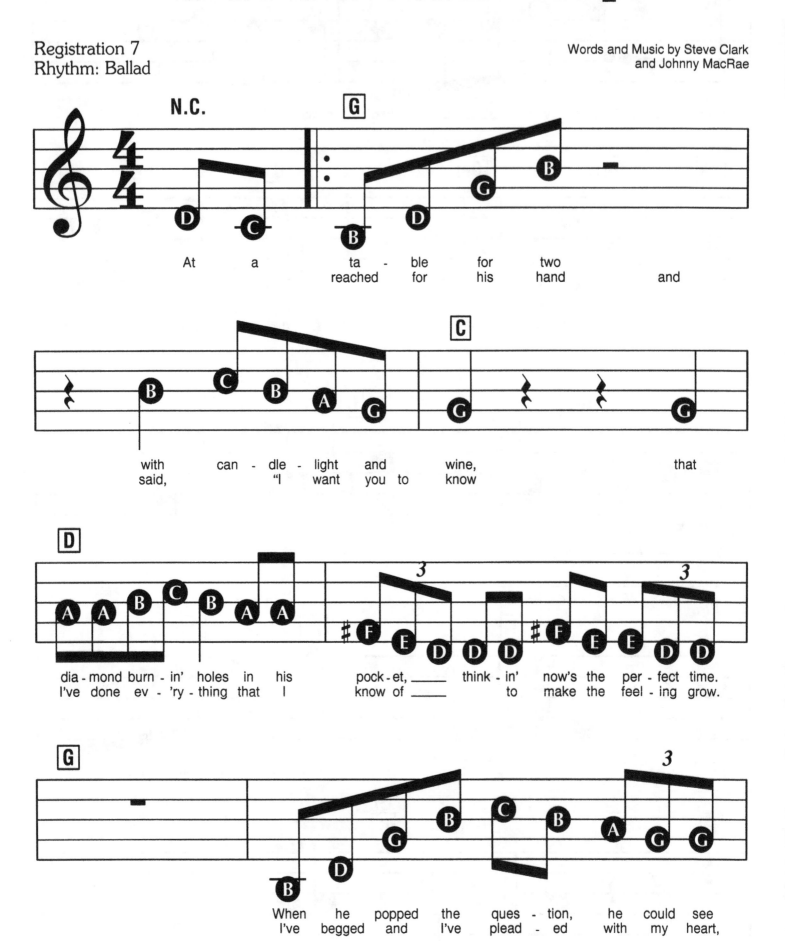

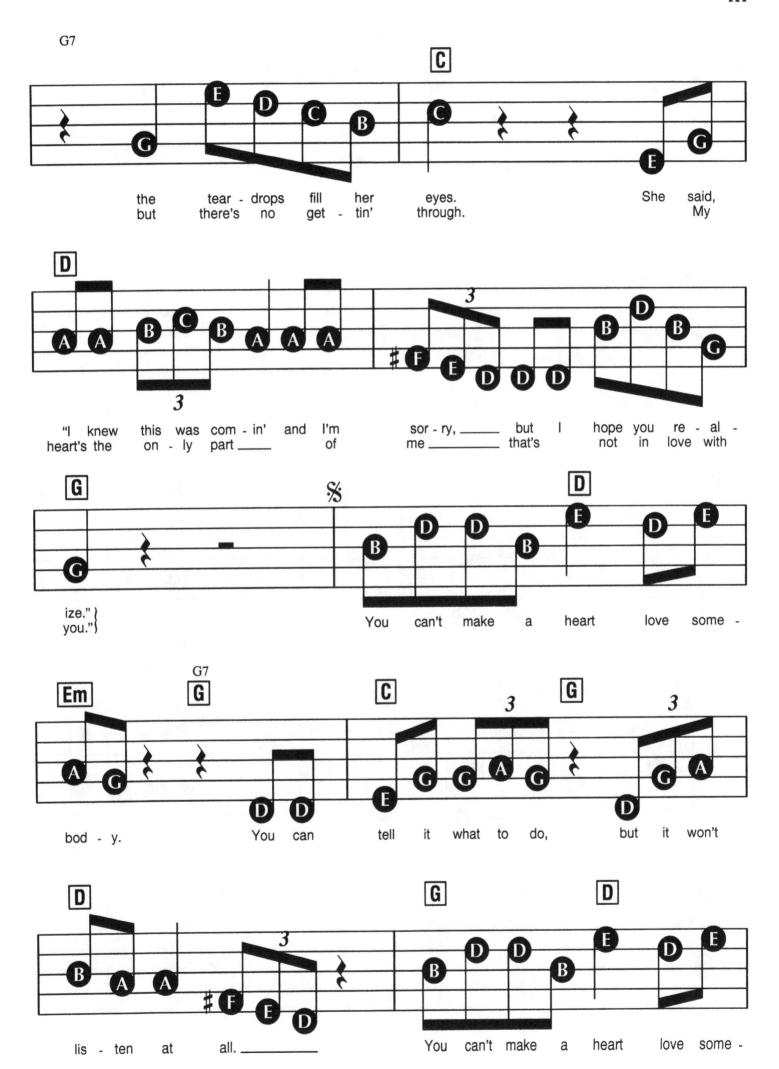

112

You Look So Good in Love

Registration 3
Rhythm: Waltz

Words and Music by Kerry Chater,
Rory Bourke and Glen Ballard

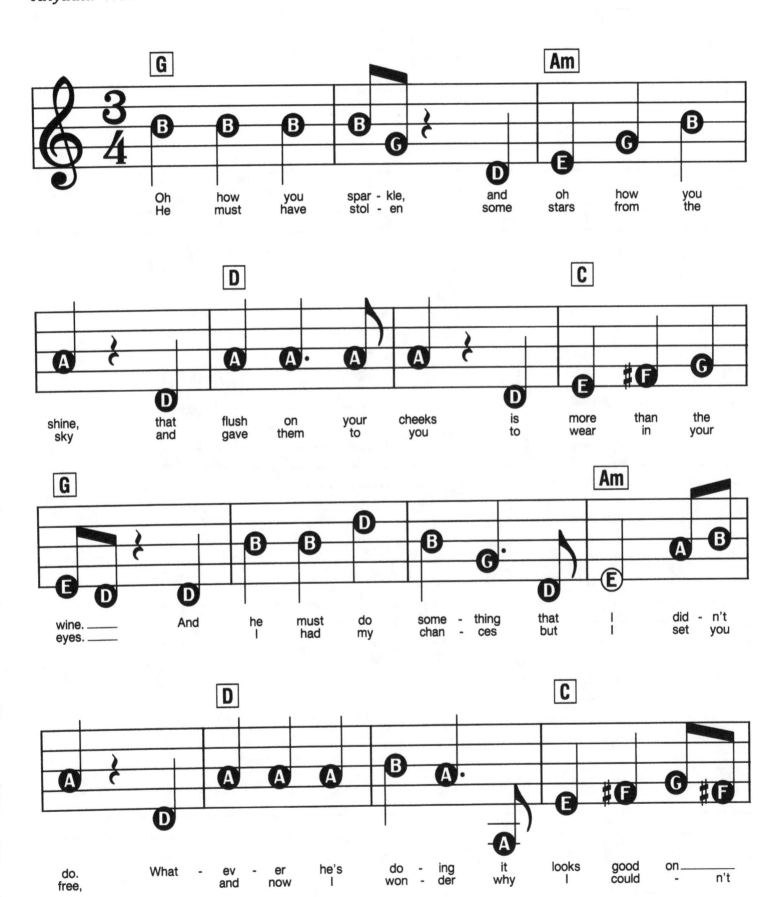

MCA music publishing

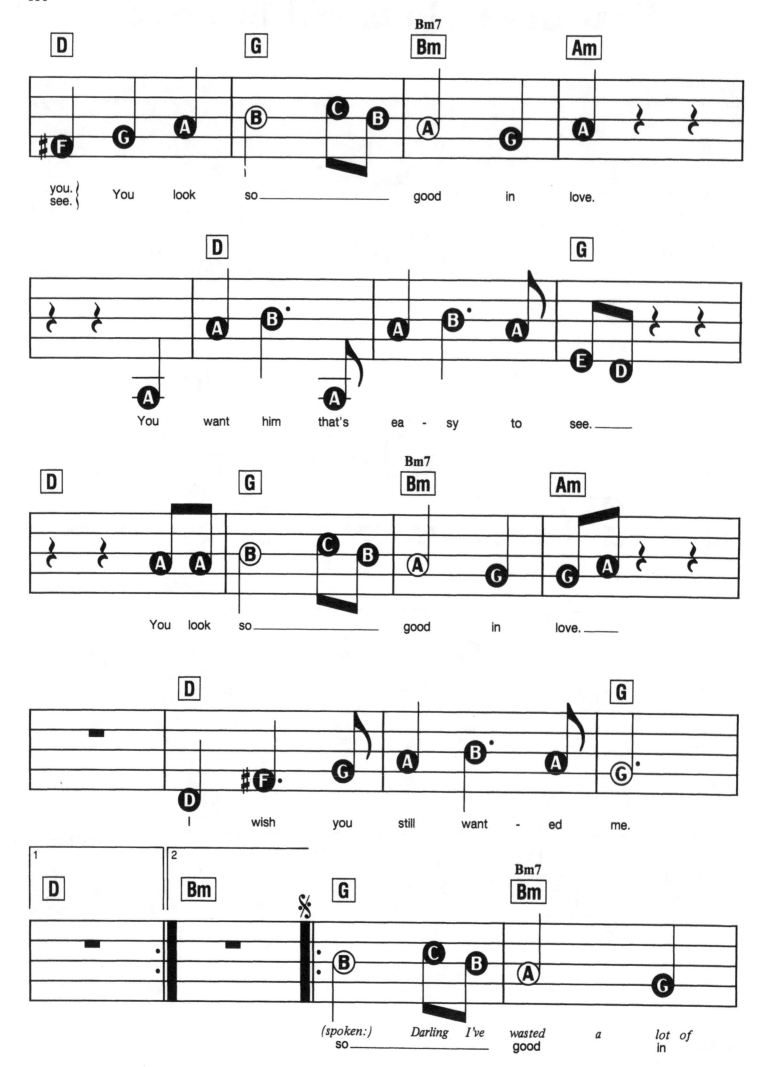

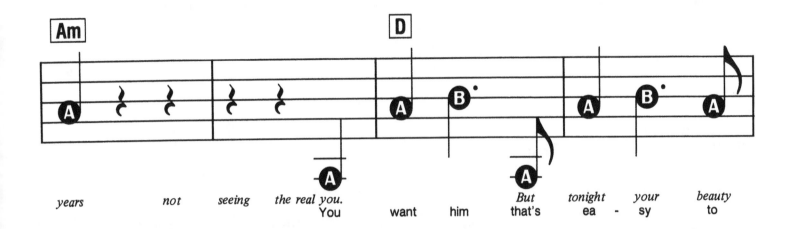

years   not   seeing   the real you.
                                        You   want   him
                                        But   that's   ea - sy   to

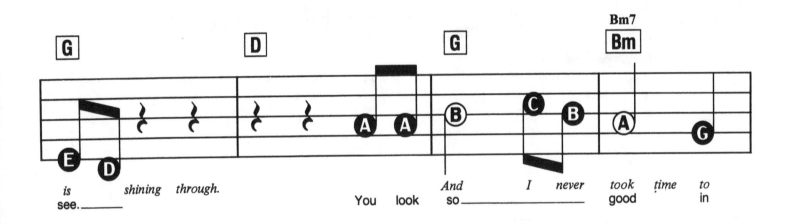

is   shining through.
see._____
                                        You   look   And   so_____   I   never   took   time   to
                                                                                                                        good   in

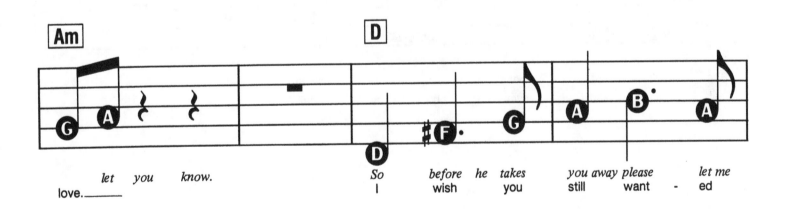

                let   you   know.
love._____
                                        So   before he takes   you away please   let me
                                        I   wish   you   still   want - ed

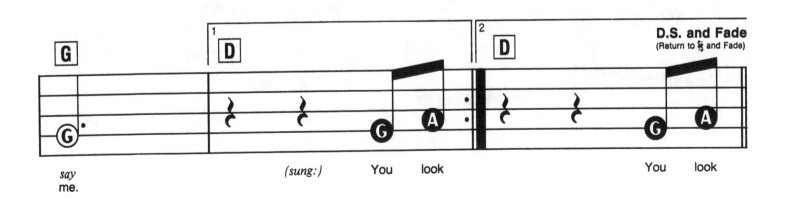

say
me.
                        (sung:)   You   look   You   look

You Know Me Better than That

Registration 9
Rhythm: Country or 16-Beat

Words and Music by Tony Haselden
and Anna Lisa Graham

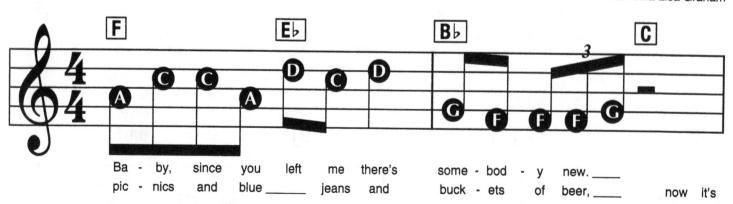

Ba - by, since you left me there's some - bod - y new. ____
pic - nics and blue ____ jeans and buck - ets of beer, ____ now it's

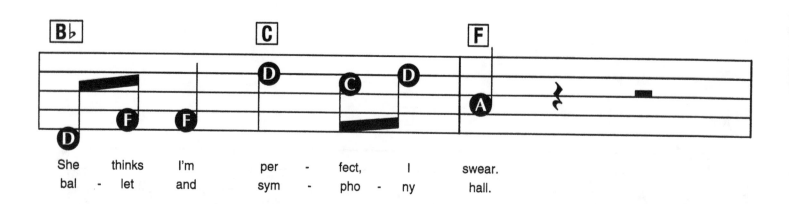

She thinks I'm per - fect, I swear.
bal - let and sym - pho - ny hall.

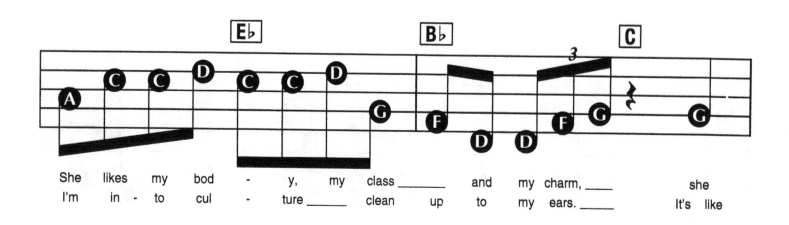

She likes my bod - y, my class ____ and my charm, ____ she
I'm in - to cul - ture ____ clean up to my ears. ____ It's like

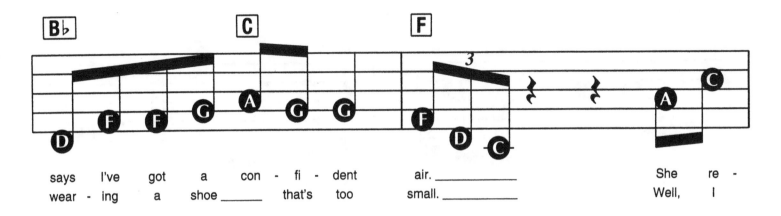

says I've got a con - fi - dent air._____ She re -
wear - ing a shoe_____ that's too small._____ Well, I

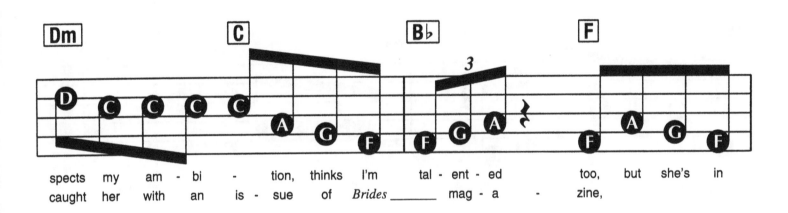

spects my am - bi - tion, thinks I'm tal - ent - ed too, but she's in
caught her with an is - sue of *Brides*_____ mag - a - zine,

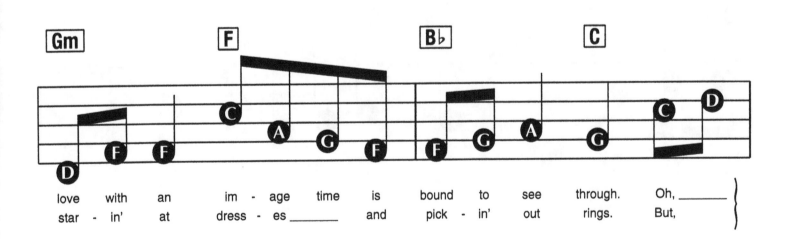

love with an im - age time is bound to see through. Oh,_____
star - in' at dress - es_____ and pick - in' out rings. But,

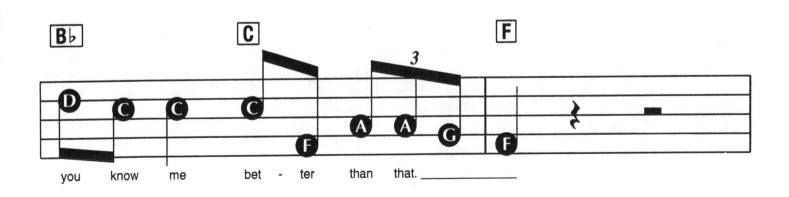

you know me bet - ter than that._____

118

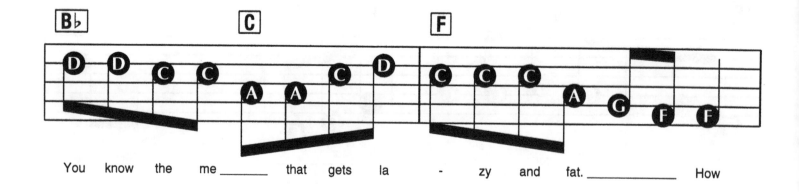

You know the me_____ that gets la - zy and fat._____ How

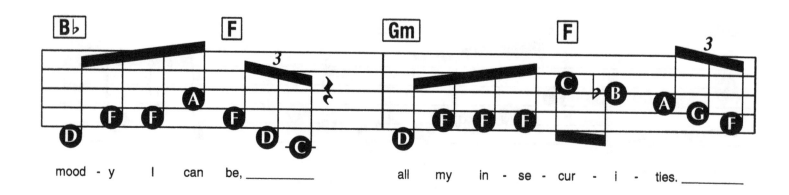

mood - y I can be,_____ all my in - se - cur - i - ties._____

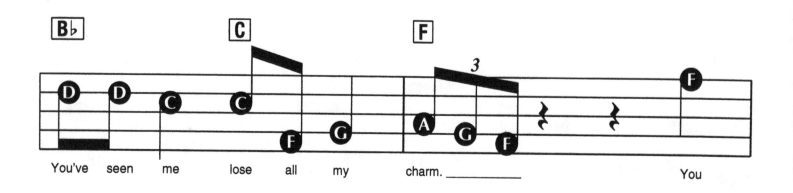

You've seen me lose all my charm._____ You

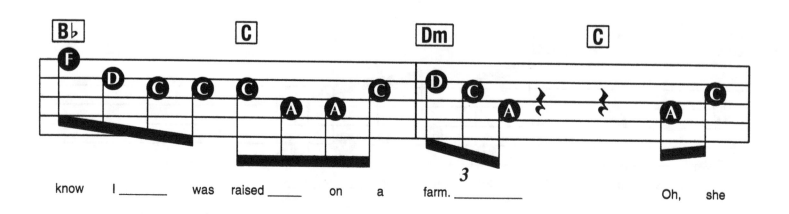

know I_____ was raised____ on a farm._____ Oh, she

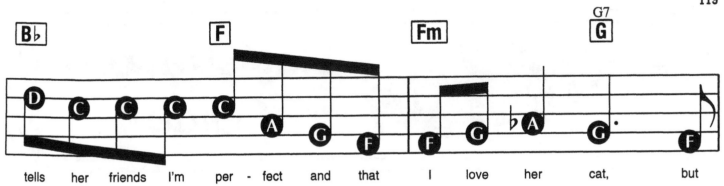

tells her friends I'm per - fect and that I love her cat, but

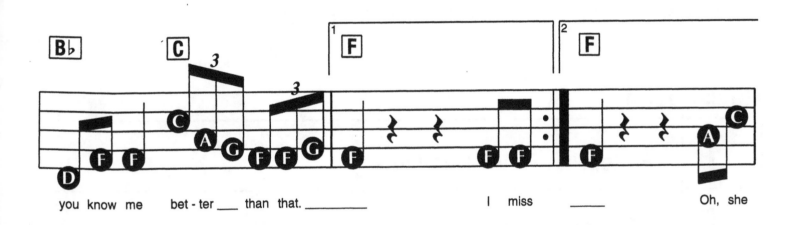

you know me bet - ter ___ than that. _____ I miss ___ Oh, she

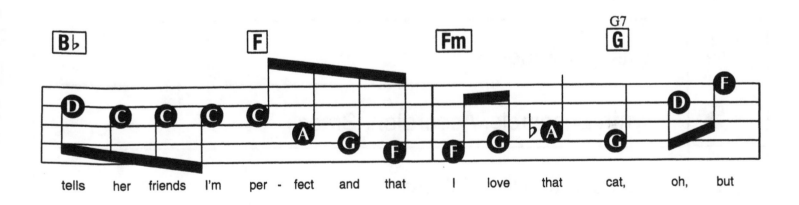

tells her friends I'm per - fect and that I love that cat, oh, but

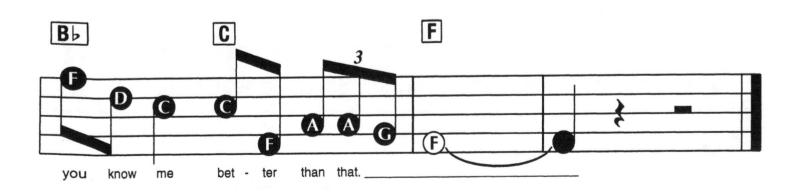

you know me bet - ter than that. _____

Registration Guide

- Match the Registration number on the song to the corresponding numbered category below. Select and activate an instrumental sound available on your instrument.

- Choose an automatic rhythm appropriate to the mood and style of the song. (Consult your Owner's Guide for proper operation of automatic rhythm features.)

- Adjust the tempo and volume controls to comfortable settings.

Registration

1	Flute, Pan Flute, Jazz Flute
2	Clarinet, Organ
3	Violin, Strings
4	Brass, Trumpet
5	Synth Ensemble, Accordion, Brass
6	Pipe Organ, Harpsichord
7	Jazz Organ, Vibraphone, Vibes, Electric Piano, Jazz Guitar
8	Piano, Electric Piano
9	Trumpet, Trombone, Clarinet, Saxophone, Oboe
10	Violin, Cello, Strings